HOW TO COOK
Complete Meals in Your
Halogen Cooker

Including extender rings and using the racks

Catherine Atkinson

foulsham

Capital Point, 33 Bath Road, Slough, Berkshire, SL1 3UF,
England

Foulsham books can be found in all good bookshops and direct from
www.foulsham.com

ISBN: 978-0-572-03755-0

Copyright © 2012 W. Foulsham & Co. Ltd

Cover photographs © top: JML (www.jmldirect.com) bottom: Fresh Food Images

A CIP record for this book is available from the British Library

The moral right of the author has been asserted

You may also be interested in:

How to cook comfort food on a tight budget
How to cook Indian

Printed and bound by CPI Group (UK) Ltd, Croydon, CR0 4YY

contents

introduction

Affordable, compact, fast and economic, the halogen cooker is a versatile kitchen appliance. It can roast, bake, grill and steam, creating flavour-packed meals with the minimum effort and fuss. Succulent roasted joints of meats, perfectly cooked fish, curries, braised vegetables, crisp-skinned baked potatoes and home-made chips; so many meals can be cooked quickly and easily with impressive results.

At around a quarter of the volume of a domestic oven, your halogen cooker will happily fit on your work surface. Its size ensures that it will heat up rapidly and it typically cooks 20–30 per cent faster than a conventional oven, saving both time and energy – yet you can still cook meals for four, including a whole roast chicken with all the trimmings. Your halogen cooker can also thaw, slow-cook and even make toast and hard-boiled eggs!

If you've just bought a halogen cooker, it will probably be accompanied by a booklet containing a handful of recipes. It may tell you how to cook a joint of meat or roast potatoes but not how to do both at the same time. This easy-to-use cookbook will show you how this is possible – and a whole lot more! It is designed to show you how make the most of your halogen cooker with complete meal recipes, each with clear step-by-step instructions. Like many other happy owners, you may find you rarely use your conventional oven again.

Here you'll find mouth-watering dishes to suit every occasion from mid-week meals to more special weekend and elegant dinner-party dining. For those who are stretched for time, there are two whole chapters devoted to dishes that can be prepared and cooked in 30 minutes or even less. Finally, for those with a sweet-tooth, you'll find a selection of delectable desserts and sweet treats. Enjoy!

Our Menu

Browse Our Menu

You'll be sure to find something to suit your mood. It's all cooked so simply that the effort won't get in the way of your enjoyment.

Our Menu

Beef

Chilli beef and garlic bread bake

A comforting retro favourite, tasty beef and plump
red kidney beans in a mildly spiced sauce,
complemented with crunchy garlic bread. *p24*

Speedy stuffed peppers

Colourful peppers, halved and lightly roasted,
then packed with lean minced meat and finished
with a bubbling cheese topping. *p26*

Chilli con carne

This classic with lean minced beef is slowly simmered
to develop all the flavours of garlic, chilli, mushrooms
and tomatoes. A generous dash of balsamic vinegar
brings it all together. *p48*

Braised beef with mustard dumplings

Full of flavour, chunks of beef together with tender
carrots and juicy green beans are topped with fluffy
dumplings with a mustard kick. *p46*

Cheat's steak and kidney pie

Slow-cooked beef and kidneys with mushrooms,
new potatoes and a dash of red wine. All topped
with a light and crisp puff pastry. *p136*

Beef and potato pasties

A tasty twist on the traditional Cornish pasty;
tiny chunks of rump steak and soft potatoes encased
in a rich, buttery pastry. *p50*

Easy beef stroganoff

Tender strips of lean steak and baby button mushrooms gently spiced with paprika. Mushroom soup, jazzed up with a drizzle of cream and seasonings, makes a simple cooking sauce. *p106*

Oriental beef with sesame noodles

Strips of tender rump steak marinated in soy and oyster sauces and cooked with fresh, crunchy vegetables and rice noodles. *p84*

Lamb

Paprika lamb cutlets with fruity couscous

Tender lamb in a sweet honey and smoky paprika glaze served simply with a date, pine nut and coriander couscous. *p28*

Easy lamb curry

Subtly blended dry spices make this curry fabulously fragrant. Perfect for entertaining friends or family. *p52*

Moroccan lamb

The tanginess of a citrus marinade marries well with lamb and chick peas and together with juicy apricots and spicy chilli gives this dish an exotic flavour. *p54*

Lamb tikka kebabs

Juicy chunks of lamb on skewers tenderised and flavoured with a tikka marinade and served with a cooling cucumber and tomato raita. *p108*

Lamb shanks with red wine

Perfect for an individual portion, lamb shanks are roasted until beautifully browned, then slowly cooked with new potatoes and leeks in a rich red wine sauce until meltingly tender. *p110*

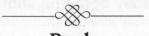

Pork

Goulash pork with dumplings
Succulent pieces of pork and tender vegetables
are bathed in a paprika sauce. Tiny bread dumplings
add a final flourish to the dish. *p56*

Pork and cider hotpot
A rich and satisfying one-pot meal with the fruity
flavour of pears and cider, enhanced with a
sliced sweet potato topping. *p58*

Apricot and pine nut pork with lemon rice
Slightly sharp dried apricots have a natural affinity
with rich meat like pork and are used here as a stuffing.
A citrus-flavoured rice is the perfect accompaniment. *p112*

Roast loin of pork with sultana stuffing
Roast pork and crunchy crackling with a sweet sultana,
tangy orange zest and herb stuffing. The addition of
roasted potatoes, parsnips and carrots make this a
memorable meal. *p114*

Creamy pork and pears
The perfect partnership of succulent pork and perfumed
pears. New potatoes, crème fraîche and a splash of cider
makes this simply delicious. *p86*

Ham and sausage

Ham and cheese calzones
A cross between a pizza and a pie, cubes of smoked
ham and melting Mozzarella are enclosed in soft and
golden bread slices. *p64*

Honey mustard gammon with corn mash
If you love strong flavours, this is the dish for you. Sticky-glazed gammon with a creamy mash jazzed up with mature Cheddar and spicy chilli. *p88*

Spinach and ricotta cannelloni
Large pasta tubes stuffed with a creamy spinach and Parma ham filling and served with garlicky mushrooms on the side. *p126*

Sausage pasta bake
A hearty supper dish combining succulent slices of sausage, cubes of melting Mozzarella and pasta shapes with a tangy tomato sauce. *p30*

Sausage and lentil braise
A satisfying supper dish of sizzling sausages and bacon bathed in a simple tomato sauce thickened with Puy lentils. *p60*

Toad in the hole with cherry tomatoes
A crisp and puffy herb batter containing meaty sausages, whole cherry tomatoes and chunks of courgette. *p62*

Chicken and turkey

Easy chicken kiev with roasted tomatoes
Chicken breasts with a garlic butter stuffing and finished with a crunchy crumb topping. Soft and juicy tomatoes complete the dish. *p32*

Creamy chicken and mushrooms
Beneath a golden topping of sliced polenta and cheese lies a layer of chunky chicken and mushrooms in a smooth creamy sauce. *p66*

Cajun chicken with cornmeal topping

The contrasting textures of spiced chicken thighs, smoky bacon and colourful peppers combined with a crunchy cornbread makes a memorable meal. *p68*

Spicy chicken balti with quinoa

So many people's favourite curry, this is accompanied with super-healthy quinoa instead of rice to ring the changes. *p70*

Chicken with mushrooms and tarragon

Lean chicken in a light and creamy tarragon sauce with baby button mushrooms is served with rice for easy entertaining. *p92*

Sticky chicken wings with herby bread

Chicken wings coated in a barbecue-style glaze and served with buttery herb bread. Finger-food at its best. *p94*

Simple chicken satay

A blend of creamed coconut and peanut butter is both marinade and sauce for strips of chicken cooked on skewers. Served in naans with cucumber and carrot. *p90*

Lemon and herb roast chicken

Classic roast chicken on a bed of braised vegetables. Ideal for Sunday lunch and a great midweek meal too. *p116*

Pot roast chicken

Moist and succulent chicken basted with parsley butter. *p118*

Italian stuffed chicken

Easy to make, chicken breasts filled with Mascarpone, olives and garlic, served with herb-scented potatoes. *p120*

Herby chicken thighs with potato cakes

Inexpensive and tasty chicken thighs, braised with a splash of white wine and accompanied with browned spring onion flavoured potato cakes. *p122*

Tandoori chicken with coriander naans

Much closer to authentic tandoori chicken than you can make in a conventional oven and served with freshly flavoured naan breads. *p124*

Turkey and leek cobbler pie

Much subtler than onions, leeks are the predominant flavour here, teamed with turkey breast and celery in a cream sauce. A scone topping perfects the dish. *p72*

Turkey and apple pittas

Minced turkey makes a welcome change from beef. Mixed with grated apples for moistness and flavour, these make fantastically healthy fast food. *p96*

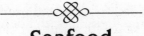

Seafood

Tuna mayo melts

Sweet red peppers, aromatic spring onions and tasty tuna combine with cheese to make a moreish pizza-style topping for crusty French bread. *p34*

Salmon with ratatouille

A bolder way to serve salmon, fillets are baked on a bed of well-flavoured red onions, peppers, courgettes and aubergine in a thick tomato sauce. *p74*

Luxury fish pie

A family favourite brought up to date with haddock, prawns, peas and sweetcorn all cooked in the simplest cream cheese sauce. *p76*

Steamed prawn and pork dumplings

An oriental dish with all the takeaway flavours but so much healthier. Wonton wrappers with a prawn and pork filling are steamed, then served with noodles. *p128*

Mixed fish casserole

This colourful dish contains the classic combination of tomatoes, onions, olives and peppers to give a distinctive Mediterranean flavour. *p130*

Spiced fish

Lemon grass, chilli, ginger and turmeric are the signature flavours of this fish dish that is cooked in foil to seal in all the juices. *p132*

Vegetarian

Spicy vegetables with lemon bulghar

Aubergines, peppers and courgettes coated in an intensely flavoured dressing with hot harissa are roasted to enhance their delicious sweetness. *p42*

Mexican bean burgers

Moist and spicy veggie burgers are gently spiced and drizzled with light citrus dressing for a delicious finish. *p36*

Red onion and asparagus frittata

Slightly caramelised sweet red onions and delicate asparagus complement each other in this Italian-style omelette. *p38*

Cauliflower and broccoli cheese

A deliciously different version of this family favourite; broccoli adds both colour and flavour to the dish. *p40*

Vegetable moussaka

A contemporary version of this Greek classic that brings all the fabulous flavours, but without the meat. *p78*

Cheese and tomato filled aubergines
The name says it all – a quick and simple Greek-inspired dish with luscious aubergines and other delightfully sunny Mediterranean flavours. *p80*

Roasted vegetables with chick pea bulghar
Delicious roasted onion, peppers and tomatoes, served with bulghar wheat and chick peas for a protein-packed veggie meal. *p98*

Cherry tomato and cheese tart
A pizza-like tart with a base of crisp puff pastry simply topped with red pesto, cherry tomatoes and two different cheeses. *p100*

Grilled vegetable bake
This is similar to a quiche but without the pastry. Mediterranean vegetables are cooked in a savoury egg, almond and Gruyère cheese custard. *p102*

Glamorgan brunch
A vegetarian alternative to a cooked English breakfast; cheese and leek sausages are served with roasted mushrooms and tomatoes. *p134*

Desserts

Tropical fruit crumble
Pineapple and bananas flavoured with rum and a crunchy coconut and brown sugar topping make an up-to-date version of everyday crumble. *p140*

Sticky syrup sponges
Light little puddings soaked in syrup and cooked by both baking and steaming to keep them beautifully moist. *p142*

Saucy lemon pudding

This well-known classic dessert separates into a rich and creamy citrus custard, topped with a light and airy sponge. *p144*

Berries and cream meringues

Perfect white meringues with crisp outer shells and marshmallow-like middles. Delicious paired with vanilla-scented cream and summer berries. *p146*

Pear puffs with streusel topping

Light layers of flaky puff pastry topped with succulent pears and sprinkled with a crumbly topping spiced with cinnamon. *p148*

White chocolate and raspberry muffins

The perfect contrast to tangy raspberries, chunks of white chocolate add extra sweetness to these light-as-air muffins. *p150*

Frosted carrot cake

A moist carrot cake, made with sunflower oil, for when you long for some cake smothered in icing but want a (relatively!) healthy treat. *p152*

Dark chocolate cake

Wickedly rich-tasting to satisfy even the most self-indulgent chocoholic, this is finished with a simple dusting of icing sugar. *p154*

Cinnamon rock cakes

Packed with dried fruit, these are a cross between a cake and a cookie and are especially delicious served while still warm. *p156*

how the halogen cooker works

The halogen cooker is basically a large glass bowl with an electric lid containing a powerful infrared halogen element and fan, temperature settings and a timer. The halogen element heats up the oven almost instantly, making it more cost-efficient than a conventional cooker as pre-heating is rarely necessary. The fan then circulates the hot air, distributing heat more efficiently from top to bottom and allowing the sides and the base of the food to cook. In many ways the combination of the halogen element and the fan makes it like a cross between an oven and a grill – the heat is highest at the top, so food at the bottom cooks more slowly. This is fantastic for foods such steaks, sausages and roasted vegetables and gives a wonderful browned topping to cheese and pastries. Other dishes such as casseroles and braises, cakes and puddings cook successfully in the halogen cooker, but will probably need to be covered with a lid or foil for at least some of the cooking time.

The glass bowl gives you a bird's eye view of what is happening inside, allowing you to monitor food without lifting the lid. Not only does this mean that heat (and therefore electricity) isn't wasted but you also don't have to constantly open the oven to see how your dish is progressing.

choosing the right machine for you

There are several different models of halogen cooker on the market. They are basically the same machine with a couple of variations; the bowl size and whether the lid is hinged or completely removable. The toughened glass bowl is usually 30–33 cm/12–13 in across and about 18 cm/7 in deep. Whether you buy an oven with a removable or a hinged lid is very much down to personal preference. Many halogen cooker cooks feel that the hinged lid is a safer and easier option and if you have a removable lid you will also need to purchase a lid stand. For safety reasons, a removable lid's handle has to be securely in place for the machine to run so that, when you lift the lid, the oven is automatically turned off. If you have a model with a hinged lid, you may have to press a start button to switch the machine on and will need to remember to turn the machine off when you lift the lid. Some ovens also have a 3-speed fan and preheat setting.

Halogen cookers are generally supplied with the following equipment:
- a glass bowl
- a base stand
- a glass lid with halogen element, timer and temperature controls and a power cord
- a steel rack
- steel handles (like tongs) so that you can safely remove oven trays.

extra equipment and accessories for your cooker

Many halogen cookers are supplied with additional items such as baking trays and extender rings. If not, you can buy these – and many other items of equipment specifically designed for use in the halogen cooker – either individually or as an accessory pack.

Steel racks

All halogen cookers are supplied with at least one rack, though most provide two; both are essential if you are planning to use your halogen cooker regularly. The shorter, low rack raises food and cooking dishes about 2.5 cm/1 in from the bottom of the bowl, allowing hot air to circulate around the food and cook it faster. This is quicker than cooking food directly in the bowl, although you can do this if you want. The taller high rack will position food closer to the element, useful for cooking foods such as steak or sausages or for browning a topping. The high and low racks can be used alone or together to increase the number of dishes you can cook at the same time.

Round baking tray

About 25 cm/10 in diameter, this essential piece of equipment is usually non-stick and may be completely flat or with very slight ridges in concentric circles.

Perforated crisping tray/steamer

About 25 cm/10 in diameter, this is usually aluminium with dozens of 5 mm/¼ in holes all over the base. This can be used for cooking pizzas or reheating pastries (the holes allow hot air to reach the base of the food) or for steaming foods such as vegetables and fish.

Extender ring

A large, sturdy metal ring about 7.5 cm/3 in deep, this fits between the top of the oven and the lid and allows you to cook large pieces of meat such as a whole chicken and deeper cakes as it keeps the halogen element further from the food. Make sure you position this the right way up – the widest part should go at the top.

Pan stand

You may want to consider buying this if you don't have a hinged-lid halogen cooker. In theory, you can put your lid on the work surface, as the element switches off automatically when the lid is lifted, but it can get very hot during long use and it is safer and easier to keep it on the stand.

Toasting racks

These can cook up to 10 slices of toast in one go and many have indents where you can cook your 'boiled' egg at the same time. Make sure you buy a rack that fits your cooker.

getting started

When positioning your halogen cooker, make sure there is plenty of clear space around it. While it occupies a space of around 40 x 40 cm/16 x 16 in, you'll need space for the lid stand (if your cooker isn't hinged) and for placing cooked foods. You also need a bit of room above the cooker so that you can easily take the lid off and for lifting out food.

1 To set up the oven, place the glass bowl on the metal base. Plug into a nearby socket. Add the metal rack(s) you require and the extender ring, if using.

2 Fit the lid on to the glass bowl or on to the extender ring and push down the handle to lock it.

3 Turn the timer clockwise to select the required time (the power light will now be on).

4 Turn the temperature dial clockwise to the required temperature. The temperature light will come on until the oven has reached the required temperature, then turn off.

5 As you cook, the temperature light will switch on and off. This is perfectly normal and not a fault with your oven.

6 If you need to lift the lid to test the food, the timer will stop automatically. When you put the lid back on and put the handle back down, the oven will turn back on and resume cooking; there is no need to reset the temperature or timer.

7 When the food has cooked for the time set, the timer bell will ring and the oven will automatically switch off. If you need to cook the food for longer, simply turn the timer back on and it will start cooking again. When the food is ready, lift up the handle (you don't need to turn off the timer or temperature) and remove the lid. The lid and oven (and extender ring if used) will be hot, so use oven gloves or the steel handles to carefully remove the food.

8 Your oven may need cleaning after use. Wipe the lid with a soapy brush or sponge, then wipe clean with a soft damp cloth (never immerse the lid in water or get the element wet). Wash the bowl by hand or in the dishwasher. Most halogen cookers have a self-cleaning function by which you add a squirt of washing up liquid to around 5 cm/2 in of hot water in the bowl and switch on to Thaw, Wash or Cleaning for 10 minutes, then rinse in clean water.

hints and tips

- In most recipes, preheating is unnecessary as the halogen cooker will reach the desired temperature in minutes. Exceptions to this are when baking cakes – notably muffins, which need to go into a hot oven so that they rise before the mixture begins to set – and hard-'boiled' eggs. The recipes in this book indicate when preheating is necessary.

- Some dishes are covered with foil for all or part of cooking to prevent the top from over-browning before the food is cooked through. Sometimes pierced foil is used; simply make a few tiny holes in it with a skewer to allow hot air to penetrate and steam to escape. When using foil, cover tightly or it may loosen as the fan circulates the air.

- Always check that food such as meat and cakes are completely cooked, because halogen cookers tend to brown the outside of food quite quickly before cooking it through.

- You can buy round baking (cookie) sheets and roasting tins specifically for your halogen cooker, but if you prefer you can always cover one of the racks with kitchen foil.

- Check that the dish you use will fit in the halogen cooker. Ideally there should be at least a 2.5 cm/1 in gap between the dish and the oven wall to allow hot air to circulate.

- Most halogen cookers have a defrost facility, which allows you to cook food from frozen. When cooking frozen meals, start on the low rack, at least until the food is fully defrosted, or you may find your meal is brown and bubbling on the top and still cold in the centre.

basic recipes

Throughout this book, you'll find lots of recipes for main meals, but the halogen cooker is also ideal for cooking snacks such as cheese on toast, and bacon and eggs for breakfast.

Toast

If you buy an accessory pack, it may include a 'breakfast rack'. This looks like a toast rack with compartments for eggs. You could also use an ovenproof (metal) toast rack; make sure there is at least a 2 cm/¾ in gap between the top and the halogen lid and, if necessary, cut the slices of bread in half to fit. Don't expect the toast cooked in a special toast rack to be browned; it is often sufficiently toasted when a pale gold colour – it may even come out white! If you don't have a toast rack, you can still make toast: arrange the slices of bread on the high rack and cook at 200°C/400°F for 5–7 minutes until the toast reaches the desired colour; it should cook on both sides without the need for turning.

Cheese on toast

Arrange slices of bread on the high rack and cook at 250°C/500° F for 3 minutes. Turn the slices over and sprinkle with grated cheese (you could add sliced tomatoes or other toppings as well). Cook for 5–6 minutes or until the topping is browned and bubbling.

Bacon

Arrange the bacon rashers (slices) on the high rack (put a baking tray on the base of the oven if you want to catch the fat). Cook at 225°C/437°F for 5 minutes, then turn over and cook for 3–4 minutes or until cooked to your liking.

Sausages

Prick the sausages with a fork or the tip of sharp knife (once is enough as you don't want to lose all the juices), then arrange on the high rack. Cook at 200°C/400°F for 12–15 minutes, turning now and then so that they brown evenly.

Steak

Lightly brush with oil, then arrange on the high rack. Depending on the thickness of the steak cook, turning once, at 200°C/400°F for 8–10 minutes for rare, 10–12 minutes for medium and 12–16 minutes for well done.

Soft- or hard-boiled eggs

These are baked rather than actually 'boiled' as cooking eggs in water takes a long time in the halogen cooker. Ideally cook the eggs from room temperature rather than straight from the fridge (if from the fridge, add an extra minute to the cooking time). Preheat the oven using the preheat setting or set the temperature to 180°C/350°F for 5 minutes. Place the eggs on the high rack or breakfast rack if you have one. Cook for 6 minutes for a soft-boiled egg, 7–8 minutes for medium and 10 minutes for a hard-boiled egg. Remove with oven gloves or a clean tea towel as they will be very hot.

Jacket potatoes

Unlike microwaved jacket potatoes, these will have a crispy brown skin when cooked. If liked, rub a little oil and sea salt over the potatoes. Prick several times, then place on the low rack. Cook at 200°C/400°F for 40–50 minutes, depending on size, until they are soft in the middle and crisp outside, turning over half-way through the cooking time. Sweet potatoes cooked in the same way only take 35–40 minutes.

Roast chicken

For a medium-sized chicken, wash and prepare – if liked, add a lemon or halved onion to the cavity for flavour, and ease up the skin and push butter and herbs under. Place breast-side down on the lower rack and cook at 225°C/437°F for 25 minutes. Turn the chicken to breast-side up and reduce the temperature to 200°C/400°F. Cook for a further 30–40 minutes or until cooked. Test by piercing the thickest part with the tip of a knife; the juices should be clear.

Adapting your own recipes

Most recipes that you would usually cook in a conventional oven or on the hob can successfully be cooked in the halogen cooker. You may find that vegetables take longer to cook than meat or fish, so slice or chop these slightly thinner or smaller than you would normally. Soups do not work well in halogen cookers, nor do casseroles or sauces with a lot of liquid (but thicker versions are fine). Experiment with your favourite recipes and usual cooking temperature, but cook for a little less time. If dishes brown too quickly, move them further from the heat source by using the low rack or the extender ring, or cover with a lid or foil, or reduce the temperature a little.

notes on the recipes

- Do not mix metric, imperial and American measures. Follow one set only.
- All spoon measures are level: 1 tsp = 5 ml; 1 tbsp = 15 ml.
- American terms are given in brackets.
- The ingredients are listed in the order in which they are used in the recipe.
- Eggs are medium unless otherwise stated. If you use a different size, adjust the amount of liquid added to obtain the right consistency.
- Always wash, peel, core, seed etc. fresh foods before use. If vegetables or fruits are to be used unpeeled it states this in the recipe. Ensure that all produce is as fresh as possible and in good condition.
- Generally use medium-sized vegetables, unless the recipe indicates otherwise.
- The recipes use a mixture of fresh seasonal produce and store-cupboard, canned and frozen ingredients. You can chop and slice your own fresh onions, chillies, garlic, ginger and herbs or use ready-prepared frozen ones, pastes and purées, if you prefer.
- The use of strongly flavoured foods such as garlic and chilli depends on personal taste, so adjust accordingly.
- Can and packet sizes are approximate and depend on the particular brand.
- Vegetarian recipes are marked with a V symbol. Omit dairy products or substitute with a vegetarian alternative if you prefer. The recipes may use processed foods, so vegetarians should check the specific product labels to be certain of their suitability. Those who eat fish but not meat will find plenty of additional recipes containing seafood to enjoy.
- Most halogen oven models have Celsius temperatures only on their dials but, as a few also have Fahrenheit, the equivalent settings are also given in the recipes.

through the door and on to the table in 30 minutes

All the recipes in this book are easy to prepare, but in this chapter you'll find some of the fastest and simplest ones, designed for those days when you are too busy to spend more than 30 minutes in the kitchen. There are plenty of dishes with flavour and flair whether you prefer a spicy chilli beef dish topped with crunchy garlic bread, simple sausages and pasta with melting cheese or protein-packed Mexican-style bean burgers. The recipes here make good use of store-cupboard and ready-prepared ingredients such as canned tuna and passata (sieved tomatoes), frozen diced onions, garlic purée (paste) and ready-grated Cheddar cheese, although the 'fresh' unprepared equivalent is also given, so you can prepare your own if you have a bit more time.

These are meals you can make in minutes with your basic halogen cooker, a low and a high rack and a baking tray – this doesn't have to be one specially designed for your oven; as long as it fits, it's fine! For some dishes, the initial cooking, such as frying onions, may done on the hob to speed up the recipe, but the main part of the cooking is completed in the halogen cooker.

chilli beef and garlic bread bake

This tasty dish takes minutes to cook and the kidney beans make the meat go further, so it is economical as well.

SERVES 4
READY IN **30 MINUTES**

lean minced (ground) beef	450 g/1 lb
olive oil	15 ml/1 tbsp
frozen diced onion,	50 g/2 oz
or onion	1, finely chopped
mild chilli powder	5–10 ml/1–2 tsp
ground cumin	5 ml/1 tsp
beef stock cube	1
can of chopped tomatoes	400 g/14 oz/large
can of red kidney beans	400 g/14 oz/large, drained and rinsed
short french stick (baguette)	1
butter	50 g/2 oz/¼ cup, softened
garlic purée (paste)	10 ml/2 tsp
salt and freshly ground black pepper	

1 Brown the mince in a large non-stick frying pan over a high heat for about 2 minutes, stirring all the time to separate the grains, then tip into an ovenproof dish.

2 Heat the oil, then add the onion and fry for 3 minutes. Add the spices, crumble the stock cube over, then stir in the tomatoes, beans and 60 ml/4 tbsp of boiling water. Return the beef to the pan and cook for about a minute, stirring to mix everything together, until the mixture is steaming hot.

3 Tip the mixture into a baking dish and cook at 200°C/ 400°F on the low rack in the halogen cooker for 15 minutes until bubbling.

4 Meanwhile, cut the baguette into 2 cm/¾ in slices. Blend together the butter and garlic purée with a little salt and pepper and spread over one side of the bread slices.

5 Stir the mince, then arrange the baguette slices on top. Cook uncovered for a further 4–5 minutes or until the bread is golden-brown and crisp. Serve straight away.

speedy stuffed peppers

Halved red or yellow peppers encase minced meat in a rich tomato sauce, topped with bubbling cheese.

 SERVES 4
READY IN **30 MINUTES**

large red or yellow peppers	2 (or 1 of each)
olive oil	25 ml/1½ tbsp
frozen diced onion,	30 ml/2 tbsp
or small onion	1, finely chopped
lean minced (ground) beef or pork	350 g/12 oz
celery stick	1, finely chopped
dried mixed herbs	2.5 ml/½ tsp
garlic purée,	5 ml/1 tsp
or garlic clove	1, crushed
passata (sieved tomatoes)	175 ml/6 fl oz/¾ cup
salt and freshly ground black pepper	
ready-grated cheddar cheese	50 g/2 oz/½ cup
crusty bread	to serve

1 Cut the peppers in half lengthwise and remove the white cores and seeds. Lightly brush the skins with 10 ml/2 tsp of the oil and place skin-side up on a baking tray on the low rack. Cook in the halogen cooker at 200°C/400°F for 5 minutes.

2 Meanwhile, heat the remaining oil in a frying pan over a high heat, add the onion and cook for a minute. Add the meat and celery and cook for 3 minutes, stirring all the time to break up the meat, until browned.

3 Stir in the herbs and garlic and cook for 30 seconds, then pour in the passata, season with salt and pepper and bring to the boil.

4 Turn the pepper halves to open-side up and divide the filling between them. Cover with foil and bake for a further 10 minutes or until the peppers are just tender.

5 Remove the foil, sprinkle the cheese over and cook for a further 3–4 minutes or until the cheese is browned and bubbling.

6 Serve with crusty bread.

paprika lamb cutlets with fruity couscous

Paprika adds a subtle smokiness to the dressing. Couscous with dates, pine nuts and coriander makes the perfect partner.

SERVES 4
READY IN **25 MINUTES**

olive oil	45 ml/3 tbsp
red wine vinegar	45 ml/3 tbsp
clear honey	10 ml/2 tsp
salt and freshly ground black pepper	
lamb cutlets	8, trimmed
paprika	10 ml/2 tsp
couscous	225 g/8 oz/2 cups
dried dates	6, roughly chopped
baby plum tomatoes	6, halved
toasted pine nuts	60 ml/4 tbsp
fresh or frozen chopped coriander (cilantro)	45 ml/3 tbsp

1 Whisk together the oil, vinegar and honey in a medium bowl with a little salt and pepper. Pour 60 ml/4 tbsp into a smaller bowl and reserve.

2 Add the lamb to the dressing in the medium bowl and coat well, then sprinkle with the paprika. Arrange the cutlets on a baking (cookie) sheet and cook on a high rack in the halogen cooker at 200°C/400°F for 7–10 minutes or until cooked to your liking, turning half-way through the cooking time. Remove from the oven, cover with foil to keep warm and leave to rest for a few minutes.

3 While the lamb is cooking, put the couscous in a bowl and pour over 900 ml/1½ pints/3¾ cups of boiling water (or light vegetable stock, if you prefer). Stir, then cover and leave to soak for 10 minutes.

4 While the couscous is soaking, stir the dates, tomatoes, pine nuts and coriander into the reserved dressing and leave for a few minutes.

5 Stir the fruit and nut mixture into the hot couscous and spoon on to warmed plates. Place the lamb on top and serve straight away.

sausage pasta bake

Here sausages are combined with pasta, ready-made tomato sauce and melting Mozzarella to make a memorable meal.

SERVES 4
READY IN **25 MINUTES**

good-quality pork sausages	8
dried pasta such as penne	350 g/12 oz
jar of ready-made tomato-based pasta sauce	350 g/12 oz
mozzarella cheese	150 g/5 oz, diced
freshly ground black pepper	
green salad	to serve

1 Put the sausages on a baking tray on the upper rack of the halogen cooker. Cook at 200°C/400°F for 6–8 minutes, turning twice during cooking, until lightly browned.

2 Meanwhile, cook the pasta in lightly salted boiling water for 10 minutes or according to the packet instructions until tender. Drain well.

3 Pour the pasta sauce into the pan and bring to the boil. Meanwhile, transfer the sausage to a board lined with kitchen paper (paper towels) and blot off the excess fat. Cut into bite-sized pieces.

4 Stir the pasta, sausage pieces and about half the Mozzarella into the sauce. Season with pepper and carefully stir together.

5 Tip into a deep casserole dish (Dutch oven) and scatter the remaining Mozzarella over the top. Cook on the low rack at 250°C/500°F for 5 minutes or until the sauce is piping hot and the cheese is melted and bubbling.

6 Serve with a green salad.

easy chicken kiev with roasted tomatoes

Traditional chicken Kiev is always deep-fried but this deliciously simple alternative gives you the same mouthwatering flavours.

SERVES 4
READY IN **30 MINUTES**

skinless chicken supremes (breasts with the wingbone attached)	4
white breadcrumbs	50 g/2 oz/1 cup
butter	75 g/3 oz/⅓ cup, softened
garlic cloves,	2, crushed
or garlic purée (paste)	10 ml/2 tsp
olive oil	30 ml/2 tbsp
cherry tomatoes on the vine	225 g/8 oz
salt and freshly ground black pepper	
ciabatta bread and a baby leaf salad	to serve

1 Make a slit along the side of each chicken breast to form a pocket. Mix 30 ml/2 tbsp of the breadcrumbs with the butter and garlic and season with a little salt and pepper. Spoon a quarter of the mixture into each chicken breast, then gently squeeze the edges of the chicken together to enclose.

2 Put the remaining breadcrumbs on a plate. Brush about 5 ml/1 tsp of the oil over the top each chicken breast, then press into the breadcrumbs. Arrange, breadcrumb-side down, in a deep baking dish.

3 Arrange the tomatoes on one side of the tray and drizzle with the remaining oil. Cook on the low rack of the halogen cooker at 180°C/350°F for 15 minutes.

4 Carefully turn the chicken over. Cook for a further 5–10 minutes or until the chicken is cooked through and the crumb topping is browned. Remove the chicken from the oven, cover with the foil and allow to rest for 2–3 minutes.

5 While the chicken is resting, warm the ciabatta in the halogen cooker for 2–3 minutes, then slice thickly.

6 Serve the chicken with the ciabatta, tomatoes and a green salad.

tuna mayo melts

French bread sliced and spread with tuna mixed with mayonnaise, yoghurt, chopped pepper and spring onions.

SERVES 4
READY IN **25 MINUTES**

french stick (preferably part-baked)	1
can of tuna	200 g/7 oz/small, drained
mayonnaise	30 ml/2 tbsp
plain yoghurt	30 ml/2 tbsp
salt and freshly ground black pepper	
red (bell) pepper	½, seeded and diced
spring onions (scallions)	2, finely sliced
large slices of cheese such as cheddar	4
salad	to serve

1 Cut the bread in half widthways, then trim if necessary to make sure the pieces will fit in the halogen cooker. Cut each piece in half lengthways.

2 Put the tuna, mayonnaise, yoghurt and a little salt and pepper in a bowl and briefly stir together. Add the red pepper and spring onions and mix well.

3 Put the bread pieces, cut-side down, on a baking tray on the low rack in the halogen cooker. Cook on 250°C/500°F for 3–4 minutes or until lightly toasted.

4 Spread the tuna mayo mixture on the untoasted (cut) side of the bread, then top with the cheese slices. Cook for a further 5–6 minutes or until the cheese is lightly browned and bubbling.

5 Serve with salad.

mexican bean burgers

These burgers should appeal to vegetarians and meat-eaters alike. The light citrus dressing brings out all the flavours.

MAKES 4
READY IN 30 MINUTES

cans of red kidney beans	2 x 400 g/14 oz/large, drained and rinsed
fresh breadcrumbs	150 g/5 oz/2½ cups
mild chilli powder	10 ml/2 tsp
fresh or frozen chopped coriander (cilantro)	45 ml/3 tbsp
egg	1, lightly beaten
tub of fresh tomato salsa	200 g/7 oz
salt and freshly ground black pepper	
greek-style yoghurt	150 ml/¼ pint/⅔ cup
fresh or bottled lime juice	15 ml/1 tbsp
wholemeal or white burger buns	4
salad leaves and sliced avocado	to serve

1 Tip the beans into a bowl and crush with a potato masher until fairly smooth. Add the breadcrumbs, chilli, 30 ml/2 tbsp of the coriander, the egg and 30 ml/ 2 tbsp of the salsa. Season with salt and pepper, then mix together.

2 Divide the mixture into four equal pieces, then shape into burgers with wet hands. Place on an oiled baking tray.

3 Cook on the low rack for 7–8 minutes or until the tops are lightly browned. Turn the burgers over and cook for a further 7–8 minutes or until lightly browned and cooked through.

4 While the burgers are cooking, mix together the yoghurt, lime juice and remaining coriander. Cut the burger buns open with a serrated knife.

5 Spread a little of the lime yoghurt over the bottom halves of the buns. Top with some salad leaves, followed by a burger, a few avocado slices, then the remaining lime yoghurt and salsa. Finish with the top burger bun half and serve straight away.

red onion and asparagus frittata

Roasting until slightly caramelised brings out all the sweet flavours of red onions; perfect for combining with asparagus.

SERVES 4
READY IN 25 MINUTES

V

thin asparagus spears	1 bunch, trimmed
olive oil	30 ml/2 tbsp
salt and freshly ground black pepper	
red onion	1, thinly sliced
balsamic vinegar	5 ml/1 tsp
eggs	8
mature cheddar cheese	50 g/2 oz, grated

1 Cut the asparagus in half and put them in a round baking tray measuring about 23 cm/9 in across. Drizzle 15 ml/1 tbsp of the oil over and season with salt and pepper. Mix well to coat evenly in the oil. Cook on a high rack in the halogen cooker at 200°C/400°F for 4 minutes, turning once.

2 Meanwhile toss the onion slices in the remaining oil and the balsamic vinegar. Add to the asparagus and cook for 5 minutes, stirring half-way through the cooking time.

3 While the vegetables are cooking, beat together the eggs with a fork, season with a little salt and pepper and stir in the cheese.

4 Add the eggs to the tray, tilting to spread out evenly. Cook for a further 4–5 minutes or until the eggs are just cooked through. Serve hot, at room temperature or cold, cut into wedges.

cauliflower and broccoli cheese

A tasty way to eat a good helping of fresh vegetables. The béchamel sauce recipe is useful if you prefer home-made.

SERVES 4
READY IN **25 MINUTES**

small cauliflower	1, cut into large florets
broccoli	225 g/8 oz, cut into large florets
béchamel sauce, bought or home-made (see opposite)	600 ml/1 pint/2½ cups
dijon mustard	5 ml/1 tsp
freshly ground black pepper	
grated cheddar cheese	75 g/3 oz/¾ cup
buttered toast	to serve

1 Bring a pan of lightly salted boiling water to the boil on the hob. Add the cauliflower and broccoli and cook for 4–5 minutes until just tender. Drain well and tip into a shallow ovenproof dish.

2 Meanwhile, heat the béchamel sauce in the pan with the mustard and a little black pepper. Bring to boiling point, stirring occasionally, then turn off the heat and stir in half the cheese. Pour over the cauliflower and broccoli and sprinkle with the rest of the cheese.

3 Put on the high rack in the halogen cooker and cook at 225°C/437°F for 7–8 minutes or until the cheese has melted and is lightly browned.

4 Serve hot with buttered toast.

Handy tip

For a home-made all-in-one béchamel sauce, blend 25 g/ 1 oz/¼ cup of plain (all-purpose) flour in a saucepan with a little milk from 600 ml/1 pint/2½ cups. Gradually stir in the rest of the milk. Add a bay leaf, a knob of butter and a little salt and ground black pepper to taste, then cook over a high heat, whisking constantly, until the mixture boils and thickens. Turn off the heat and remove the bay leaf.

spicy vegetables with lemon bulghar

This dish is given flavour by roasting aubergines, peppers and courgettes in a blend of hot harissa paste, honey and oil.

SERVES 4
READY IN **30 MINUTES**

lemon	1
olive oil	45 ml/3 tbsp
clear honey	30 ml/2 tbsp
harissa paste	15 ml/1 tbsp
salt and freshly ground black pepper	
small aubergine (eggplant)	1, halved and cut into wedges
red or yellow (bell) pepper	1, seeded and cut into chunks
courgette (zucchini)	1, cut into 2 cm/¾ in slices
bulghar (cracked wheat)	225 g/8 oz/2 cups
chopped fresh mint (optional)	15 ml/1 tbsp
plain yoghurt or soya yoghurt	60 ml/4 tbsp

1 Pare a strip of zest from the lemon, squeeze out the juice and reserve.

2 Put a roasting tin or baking tray in the halogen cooker, then preheat using the preheat setting or set the temperature to 200°C/400°F. Whisk together the oil, honey, lemon juice and harissa in a large bowl and season with a little salt and pepper. Set aside 15 ml/ 1 tbsp of the dressing, then add the vegetables to the rest in the bowl and toss well to mix.

3 Tip the vegetables into the roasting tin and cook for 20 minutes, turning once or twice during cooking, or until tender and lightly charred.

4 Meanwhile, put the bulghar in a heatproof bowl. Add the strip of lemon zest, then pour over enough boiling water to cover the bulghar by about 5 cm/2 in. Cover and leave to soak for 15 minutes. Drain well, discard the lemon zest, tip back into the bowl and cover to keep warm.

5 Add the roasted vegetables to the bulghar and mix together. Stir the remaining dressing into the yoghurt with the mint, if using. Drizzle over the bulghar and vegetables and serve hot.

meals from your basic oven

Here you'll find a selection of recipes that are straightforward and easy to follow and don't need extra accessories or equipment. If you are new to the halogen cooker this is a good place to start. Nothing could be easier to prepare than a whole meal cooked in one dish, well balanced nutritionally and with the minimum of fuss.

Ideas include braised beef topped with fluffy mustard-flavoured dumplings, a simple but aromatic lamb curry and a vegetarian version of moussaka. For those with big appetites, you could add some crusty bread and, to ensure you get your 'five-a-day', a bag of ready-prepared salad or some quickly cooked peas or sweetcorn will add the finishing touch to your delicious meal.

braised beef with mustard dumplings

Here lean beef is combined with onions and carrots, with green beans added towards the end of cooking.

SERVES 4
READY IN **2 HOURS**

lean braising or chuck steak	450 g/1 lb, trimmed and cut into 5 cm/2 in cubes
cornflour (cornstarch)	30 ml/2 tbsp
ground allspice	1.5 ml/¼ tsp
onion	1, thinly sliced
large carrots	2, thickly sliced
garlic cloves,	2, crushed
or garlic purée (paste)	10 ml/2 tsp
green beans	200 g/7 oz, cut into 2.5 cm/1 in lengths
bay leaf	1
salt and freshly ground black pepper	
tomato purée	30 ml/2 tbsp
balsamic vinegar	15 ml/1 tbsp
boiling beef stock	600 ml/1 pint/2½ cups
For the mustard dumplings:	
self-raising flour	175 g/6 oz/1½ cups
butter	50 g/2 oz/¼ cup, diced
dijon mustard	10 ml/2 tsp

1 Toss the beef in a mixture of the cornflour and allspice. Put it in a deep ovenproof dish (make sure there is a gap of at least 2.5 cm/1 in between the dish and the oven wall so the hot air can circulate) with the onion, carrots, garlic, beans, bay leaf, salt and pepper.

2 Stir the tomato purée and balsamic vinegar into the stock. Pour over the meat and vegetables, cover with a lid or foil, then cook on the low rack at 180°C/350°F for 1½ hours.

3 To make the dumplings, towards the end of the cooking time, put the flour and a pinch of salt and pepper in a bowl, add the butter and rub in until the mixture resembles fine breadcrumbs.

4 Mix the mustard with 30 ml/2 tbsp of cold water and add to the dry ingredients. Stir together, adding a little more water if needed to make a soft but not sticky dough. Shape into 20 small balls.

5 Place the dumpling balls on top of the beef mixture and cook, uncovered, for a further 12–15 minutes or until risen and cooked through. Serve straight away.

chilli con carne

The slow cooking of this all-time favourite comfort food allows all the flavours to develop – and no extra pans to wash up!

SERVES 4
READY IN **2¼ HOURS**

lean minced (ground) beef	450 g/1 lb
onion	1, finely chopped
garlic cloves,	2, crushed
or garlic purée (paste)	10 ml/2 tsp
chilli powder	5–10 ml/1–2 tsp
ground cumin	2.5 ml/½ tsp
plain (all-purpose) flour	15 ml/1 tbsp
hot beef stock	250 ml/8 fl oz/1 cup
tomato purée	30 ml/2 tbsp
can of chopped tomatoes	400 g/14 oz/large
mushrooms	75 g/3 oz, sliced
can of red kidney beans	400 g/14 oz/large, drained and rinsed
dried oregano or mixed herbs	5 ml/1 tsp
salt and freshly ground black pepper	
crusty bread	to serve

1 Put the beef and onion in a large ovenproof dish that fits in the halogen oven (make sure there is a gap of at least 2.5 cm/1 in between the dish and the oven wall so the hot air can circulate). Break up the beef with your fingers, mixing in the onion.

2 Cook uncovered on the low rack at 220°C/425°F for 20 minutes, stirring every 5 minutes, until the beef is brown and the onion is beginning to soften.

3 Stir in the garlic, then sprinkle the chilli powder, cumin and flour over. Stir well, then gradually add the stock. Stir in the tomato purée, chopped tomatoes, mushrooms, kidney beans, herbs, salt and pepper.

4 Cover the dish with a lid or foil with a few tiny holes pierced in it and cook at 180°C/350°F for 1¼–1½ hours, stirring every 30 minutes, or until the meat and onion are tender.

5 Serve with crusty bread.

beef and potato pasties

Buttery pastry packed with steak and potato. Turning them over half-way means the pastry is golden and flaky on both sides.

MAKES 4
READY IN **1¼ HOURS**

For the pastry:

plain (all-purpose) flour	225 g/8 oz/2 cups
salt and freshly ground black pepper	
chilled butter (or butter and lard or white vegetable fat)	125 g/4½ oz/generous ½ cup, diced
egg yolk	1
cold water	15 ml/1 tbsp

For the filling:

rump steak	150 g/5 oz
small potato	1, about 100 g/4 oz
small onion	½, very finely chopped
dried mixed herbs	2.5 ml/½ tsp
salad and coleslaw	to serve

1 To make the pastry, sift the flour and a pinch of salt into a bowl. Rub in the fat until the mixture resembles fine breadcrumbs. Mix together the egg yolk and water, then sprinkle over the dry ingredients and mix to a soft dough. Knead the pastry on a lightly floured surface for a few seconds until smooth. Wrap in clingfilm (plastic wrap) and chill in the fridge for 20 minutes.

2 Meanwhile, to make the filling, chop the beef and potato into small pieces and put in a bowl with the onion, herbs, salt and pepper. Mix well.

3 Divide the pastry into four pieces, then roll out each piece on a lightly floured surface to a 15 cm/6 in round. Spoon an equal amount of filling on to one half of each pastry round. Brush the pastry edges with water, then fold the other half over the filling. Press the edges firmly together to seal and crimp the edges.

4 Transfer the pastries to a baking tray and cook on the low rack at 180°C/350°F for 15 minutes. Turn the pastries over and cook for a further 15 minutes.

5 Cover the pastries with a piece of foil, pierced several times with a skewer to allow steam to escape, and reduce the temperature to 160°C/325°F. Bake for a further 15 minutes.

6 Serve hot or cold with salad and coleslaw.

easy lamb curry

Forget your craving for takeaway! This lamb curry cooked in a rich, mildly spicy sauce is a dish worth staying in for.

SERVES 4
READY IN 1¼ HOURS

ghee or unsalted (sweet) butter	25 g/1 oz/2 tbsp
sunflower oil	30 ml/2 tbsp
lean boneless lamb	700 g/1½ lb, trimmed and cut into 5 cm/2 in cubes
onions	2, sliced
garlic cloves,	2, crushed
or garlic purée (paste)	10 ml/2 tsp
cardamom pods	8, crushed to open
ground cumin	10 ml/2 tsp
chilli powder	10 ml/2 tsp
ground ginger	10 ml/2 tsp
garam masala	10 ml/2 tsp
beef or vegetable stock	450 ml/¾ pint/2 cups
salt	to taste
fresh or frozen chopped coriander (cilantro)	30 ml/2 tbsp
naan breads and popadoms	to serve

1 Melt the ghee or butter in a frying pan on the hob with the oil. Add the lamb and fry for 3–4 minutes until browned. Transfer to a casserole dish (Dutch oven) using a slotted spoon and leaving as much fat as possible behind in the pan (make sure the dish fits in the halogen oven with a gap of at least 2.5 cm/1 in between it and the oven wall so the hot air can circulate).

2 Add the onions to the pan and fry gently for 5 minutes until they are beginning to soften. Stir in the garlic and dry spices and cook for 1 minute more.

3 Stir in the stock and season with salt. Pour over the lamb and stir.

4 Cover with a lid or foil pierced a few times with a skewer and put on the low rack in the halogen oven. Cook at 190°C/375°F for 50–60 minutes or until the lamb and onions are tender, stirring half-way through the cooking time.

5 Stir in the coriander and serve with naan breads (these can be warmed in the halogen oven for a minute or two while serving the curry) and popadoms.

moroccan lamb

Marinating allows the flavours to penetrate and tenderises the meat, which is accompanied by lemon couscous.

SERVES 4
READY IN **1½ HOURS, PLUS MARINATING**

For the lamb:	
chilli powder	10 ml/2 tsp
ground cumin	10 ml/2 tsp
ground ginger	10 ml/2 tsp
ground cinnamon	5 ml/1 tsp
orange juice	15 ml/1 tbsp
lean lamb	550 g/1¼ lb, cut into 4 cm/1½ in cubes
small shallots	225 g/8 oz
olive oil	45 ml/3 tbsp
garlic cloves,	2, crushed
or garlic purée (paste)	10 ml/2 tsp
plain (all-purpose) flour	15 ml/1 tbsp
lamb or vegetable stock	300 ml/½ pint1¼ cups
tomato purée (paste)	15 ml/1 tbsp
salt and freshly ground black pepper	
dried apricots	100 g/4 oz, quartered
can of chick peas	400 g/14 oz/large, drained
For the couscous:	
lemon (optional)	½
couscous	225 g/8 oz/1⅓ cups
boiling vegetable stock	300 ml/½ pint/1¼ cups
chopped fresh herbs (optional)	to serve

1 To make the lamb, put the spices in a bowl with the orange juice and whisk together with a fork. Add the lamb and stir to coat all the pieces. Cover and leave to marinate in the fridge for 1–4 hours.

2 Put the shallots in heatproof bowl and pour over enough boiling water to cover. Leave for 10 minutes or until the water is tepid, then peel off the skins (they should now come away easily).

3 Heat 30 ml/2 tbsp of the oil in a large frying pan, add the shallots and fry for 3–4 minutes until golden-brown. Transfer to a casserole dish (Dutch oven) using a slotted spoon and leaving any oil behind in the pan (make sure that the dish fits in the halogen oven with a gap of at least 2.5 cm/1 in between it and the oven wall so that the hot air can circulate).

4 Drain the lamb, reserving the marinade, and pat dry with kitchen paper (paper towels). Heat the remaining oil in the pan, add the lamb and fry over a high heat for 3–4 minutes or until browned all over.

5 Add the garlic to the pan and cook for a few seconds, then sprinkle the flour over. Turn off the heat and stir in the stock a little at a time, followed by the tomato purée and reserved marinade. Season with salt and pepper and pour into the casserole. Stir in the apricots and chick peas.

6 Cover with a lid or foil and cook on the low rack in the halogen oven at 200°C/400°F for 50 minutes or until the lamb and shallots are tender.

7 Meanwhile, to make the couscous, grate the zest from the lemon, if using. Put in a bowl with the couscous and pour the boiling stock over. Cover and leave for 8–10 minutes. Fluff up with a fork and season to taste with salt and pepper. Stir in some chopped fresh herbs, if you like.

goulash pork with dumplings

Choose a mild or spicier variety of paprika for the rich, smoky tomato sauce. Tiny bread dumplings soak up the tasty cooking juices.

SERVES 4
READY IN **1½ HOURS**

sunflower oil	30 ml/2 tbsp
lean boneless pork	550 g/1¼ lb, cut into 2.5 cm/1 in cubes
large onion	1, thinly sliced
garlic cloves	2, finely chopped
carrots	2, diced
white cabbage	150 g/5 oz, finely shredded
paprika	15 ml/1 tbsp
caraway seeds	1.5 ml/¼ tsp
can of chopped tomatoes	400 g/14 oz/large
hot beef stock	600 ml/1 pint/2½ cups
salt and freshly ground black pepper	
For the topping:	
egg	1
milk	60 ml/4 tbsp
fresh white breadcrumbs	150 g/5 oz/2½ cups
chopped fresh or frozen parsley,	15 ml/1 tbsp
or dried mixed herbs	a large pinch

1 Heat 15 ml/1 tbsp of the oil in a large frying pan, add the pork and cook over a high heat for 5 minutes, stirring until browned all over. Lift out the meat with a slotted spoon, leaving any fat and juices behind, and transfer to a casserole dish (Dutch oven).

2 Heat the remaining oil in the pan, add the onion and garlic and cook over a medium heat, stirring frequently, for about 10 minutes or until beginning to brown. Add the carrots and cook, stirring, for a further 3–4 minutes.

3 Stir in the cabbage, then sprinkle the paprika and caraway seeds over and cook for a few seconds, then pour in the chopped tomatoes and heat until steaming. Tip the mixture over the pork. Stir in the stock and season with salt and pepper.

4 Cover with a lid or foil pierced a few times with a fine skewer and cook on the low rack in the halogen oven at 180°C/350°F for 45 minutes.

5 To make the dumplings, towards the end of the cooking time, beat together the egg and milk in a bowl, then add the breadcrumbs and parsley or herbs and salt and pepper to taste. Using damp hands, shape into 12 walnut-sized balls.

6 Uncover the pork and place the bread dumplings on top. Cook for 15 minutes or until the meat and vegetables are tender and the dumplings are cooked through.

pork and cider hotpot

Cooking with a little cider gives a delicious depth to the gravy, but it's still a family meal as the alcohol evaporates as it simmers.

SERVES 4
READY IN **1¾ HOURS**

lean boneless pork	550 g/1¼ lb
plain (all-purpose) flour	15 ml/1 tbsp
salt and freshly ground black pepper	
unsalted (sweet) butter	40 g/1½ oz/3 tbsp
sunflower oil	15 ml/1 tbsp
leek	1, thinly sliced
firm ripe pear or eating (dessert) apple	1, peeled, cored and thinly sliced
cider or a mixture of cider and stock	450 ml/¾ pint/2 cups
dried sage or thyme	2.5 ml/½ tsp
wholegrain mustard	15 ml/1 tbsp
crème fraîche	75 ml/5 tbsp
sweet potatoes	450 g/1 lb, peeled and thinly sliced

1 Cut the pork into bite-sized pieces, then toss in the flour seasoned with salt and pepper. Gently heat the butter with the oil in a large frying pan until melted, then remove 15 ml/1 tbsp and set aside.

2 Turn up the heat to medium high, add the pork to the pan and fry on all sides for about 3 minutes until beginning to brown, then add the leek and cook for a further 3–4 minutes.

3 Add the pear or apple slices to the pan with the cider, sage or thyme, mustard and crème fraîche. Stir over a medium heat until piping hot, then transfer to a casserole (Dutch oven) or baking dish (make sure the dish fits in the halogen oven with a gap of at least 2.5 cm/1 in between it and the oven wall so the hot air can circulate).

4 Arrange the sweet potato slices over the pork, then brush with the reserved oil and butter mixture. Cover with a lid or foil pierced a few times with a skewer and cook on a low rack in the halogen oven at 180°C/350°F for 1 hour.

5 Check that the potatoes are tender; if not, re-cover and cook for a further 10–15 minutes. Remove the lid or foil and cook uncovered for a final 10–15 minutes to allow the top to brown.

sausage and lentil braise

For this satisfying supper dish, sausages and pancetta are cooked with Puy lentils. Serve with crusty bread for big appetites.

SERVES 4
READY IN **1¼–1½ HOURS**

puy lentils	275 g/10 oz, rinsed
good-quality sausages	450 g/1 lb
cubed pancetta or diced bacon	100 g/4 oz
onion	1, chopped
carrot	1, chopped
garlic cloves,	2, crushed
or garlic purée (paste)	10 ml/2 tsp
dried thyme	2.5 ml/½ tsp
boiling vegetable stock	750 ml/1¼ pints/3 cups
red wine vinegar	10 ml/2 tsp
can of chopped tomatoes	400 g/14 oz/large
chopped fresh or frozen parsley	45 ml/3 tbsp
salt and freshly ground black pepper	

1 Put the lentils in a heatproof bowl and pour over enough boiling water to cover them by about 2 cm/ ¾ in. Leave to soak.

2 Meanwhile, prick the sausages with a fork or the tip of a sharp knife, then arrange on the high rack and put a baking tray on the low rack to catch the fat. Cook at 200°C/400°F for 10–12 minutes, turning frequently, until very lightly browned. Transfer the sausages to a plate lined with kitchen paper (paper towels) to drain off excess fat.

3 Tip most of the fat away from the baking tray, leaving about 15 ml/1 tbsp behind. Add the pancetta or bacon and the onion and cook for 3 minutes or until beginning to colour and soften, then stir in the carrot, garlic and thyme and cook for 5 minutes.

4 Tip the mixture into a casserole dish (Dutch oven), making sure the dish fits in the halogen oven with a gap of at least 2.5 cm/1 in between it and the oven wall so the hot air can circulate. Drain the lentils and stir in with the stock, vinegar and tomatoes. Add the sausages and cover with a lid or foil.

5 Cook on the low rack in the halogen oven at 180°C/350°F for 45–50 minutes or until the sausages and lentils are tender, stirring half-way through the cooking time. Stir in the parsley and season to taste with salt and pepper before serving.

toad in the hole with cherry tomatoes

Cherry tomatoes and courgettes are added to the batter with the sausages, so there's no need to add extra vegetables.

SERVES 4
READY IN **1 HOUR**

sunflower oil	15 ml/1 tbsp
courgettes (zucchini)	2, cut into 2 cm/¾ in slices
good-quality pork sausages	450 g/1 lb
cherry tomatoes	8
For the batter:	
plain (all-purpose) flour	100 g/4 oz/1 cup
salt	a pinch
eggs	2
milk	300 ml/½ pint/1¼ cups
dried thyme	2.5 ml/½ tsp

1 Use half the oil to grease a small roasting tin. Add the courgette slices and drizzle with the remaining oil, tossing to lightly coat. Add the sausages to the tin.

2 Place on the low rack in the halogen oven and cook at 200°C/400°F for 6 minutes, turning occasionally, until the sausages are lightly browned.

3 Meanwhile, to make the batter, sift the flour and salt into a bowl. Make a hollow in the middle and add the eggs with a little of the milk. Whisk the eggs and milk together, gradually incorporating the flour to make a thick paste. Beat in the rest of the milk and the herbs to make a smooth batter.

4 If there is a lot of fat in the pan from the sausages, tip some away to leave about 15 ml/1 tbsp. Pierce the tomatoes with the tip of a knife and add to the pan, spacing the sausages and vegetables evenly. Heat for 2 more minutes or until the pan is really hot.

5 Quickly and carefully pour the batter over the sausages and vegetables. Cook, still at 200°C/400°F, for 15 minutes, then lower the heat to 180°C/350°F and cook for a further 15–20 minutes or until the batter is well-risen and is a deep golden-brown. Cut into portions and serve straight away.

ham and cheese calzones

A bit like an Italian version of Cornish pasties but with smoked ham, tomato and cheese inside a quick-mix bread dough.

 MAKES 4
READY IN 40 MINUTES

tomatoes	2, chopped
smoked ham	100 g/4 oz, chopped into 1 cm/½ in cubes
mozzarella cheese	175 g/6 oz, chopped into 1 cm/½ in cubes
salt and freshly ground black pepper	
self-raising flour	225 g/8 oz/2 cups
baking powder	2.5 ml/½ tsp
milk	150 ml/¼ pint/⅔ cup
olive oil	20 ml/4 tsp, plus extra for brushing
green salad	to serve

1 Put the tomatoes, ham and Mozzarella in a bowl. Season with salt and pepper and stir together.

2 Sift the flour, baking powder and a pinch of salt into a bowl and mix. Make a hollow in the middle. Pour the milk and oil into the hollow and mix to make a soft dough. Divide the dough into four equal pieces and roll out each piece to a round about 15 cm/6 in across.

3 Spoon the filling on to one half of each the circles, dividing it equally. Brush a little water or milk around the edge. Fold the dough over the mixture and pinch along the edges to seal the two halves.

4 Place the low rack in the halogen oven and preheat to 200°C/400°F for 2–3 minutes. Brush one side of the calzones lightly with olive oil. Put on a baking tray and bake for 8 minutes until lightly browned.

5 Turn the calzones over and lightly brush the other side with olive oil. Bake for a further 8–10 minutes, lowering the heat to 175°C/340°F if they start browning too much.

6 Serve warm with a green salad.

creamy chicken and mushrooms

Polenta can be bought in a sliceable slab, and here it is used with cheese to make a topping for chicken in a creamy sauce.

SERVES 4
READY IN **1 HOUR**

frozen soya beans	150 g/5 oz
onion	1, chopped
sunflower oil	15 ml/1 tbsp
baby button mushrooms	150 g/5 oz
cream cheese	150 g/5 oz
boiling chicken stock	75 ml/5 tbsp
wholegrain mustard	5 ml/1 tsp
dried thyme	2.5 ml/½ tsp
chicken breasts	450 g/1 lb, cut into 2 cm/¾ in chunks
salt and freshly ground black pepper	
packet of ready-made polenta	500 g/18 oz, thinly sliced
parmesan or mature cheddar cheese	25 g/1 oz, finely grated

1 Spread out the soya beans on a plate lined with kitchen paper (paper towels) to defrost. Put the onion in an ovenproof dish (make sure the dish fits in the halogen oven with a gap of at least 2.5 cm/1 in between it and the oven wall so the hot air can circulate), and drizzle the oil over. Stir, then cook on the low rack in the halogen oven at 200°C/400°F for 5 minutes.

2 Add the mushrooms to the onion and stir well, then cook for a further 6–7 minutes or until the onions are just beginning to colour. Turn down the oven temperature to 175°C/340°F.

3 Add the cream cheese, stock, mustard and thyme. Stir until the cream cheese has melted, then add the chicken, soya beans, salt and pepper and mix together (the mixture will be very thick at this stage but will be thinned by the chicken and mushroom juices during cooking).

4 Arrange the polenta in overlapping slices over the chicken mixture and sprinkle the Parmesan or Cheddar cheese over. Cover with pierced foil and cook for 20 minutes. Remove the foil and cook for a further 5–10 minutes or until the cheese is browned and the chicken is cooked.

cajun chicken with cornmeal topping

Well-flavoured chicken thighs are cooked with smoky bacon and Cajun spices and covered with a light cornbread topping.

SERVES 4
READY IN **50–60 MINUTES**

chicken thighs	4 large or 8 small, skinned, boned and quartered
cajun spice blend	10 ml/2 tsp
onion	1, chopped
olive oil	15 ml/1 tbsp
smoked streaky bacon rashers (slices)	2, rinded and chopped
red (bell) pepper	1, seeded and sliced
yellow pepper	1, seeded and sliced
self-raising flour	100 g/4 oz/1 cup
polenta (cornmeal)	100 g/4 oz/1 cup
grated cheddar cheese	75 g/3 oz/¾ cup
dried chilli flakes	a pinch
butter	50 g/2 oz/¼ cup, melted
milk	100 ml/3½ fl oz/scant ½ cup
egg	1, lightly beaten

1 Put the chicken in a bowl and sprinkle the Cajun spice blend over. Mix well and set aside for a few minutes.

2 Put the onion in an ovenproof dish at least 7.5 cm/3 in deep (make sure there is a gap of at least 2.5 cm/1 in between the dish and the oven wall so the hot air can circulate). Drizzle with the oil, then mix until well coated. Put on the low rack in the halogen oven and heat to 250°C/500°F. Cook for 4–5 minutes or until the onion is starting to soften.

3 Add the bacon and peppers and mix again. Cook for 8 minutes, stirring once half-way through the cooking time. Set the chicken pieces on top of the bacon and vegetables and cook for 5 minutes or until lightly browned.

4 Meanwhile, mix together the flour, polenta, cheese and chilli flakes in a bowl. Make a hollow in the middle of the dry ingredients. Mix together the butter, milk and egg and pour into the hollow. Stir with a fork to make a sticky dough, then drop spoonfuls over the top of the chicken mixture.

5 Return the dish to the oven and cook for 5 minutes, then lower the temperature to 200°C/400°F and cook for a further 10–12 minutes or until the topping is well browned and cooked through.

spicy chicken balti with quinoa

Cooked quinoa has a texture similar to lentils. It makes a great alternative to rice in this well-known chicken curry dish.

SERVES 4
READY IN 1 HOUR

sunflower oil	30 ml/2 tbsp
onions	2, thinly sliced
skinless chicken breasts	4
balti curry paste	60 ml/4 tbsp
quinoa	225 g/8 oz/2 cups
can of chopped tomatoes	400 g/14 oz/large
chicken or vegetable stock	900 ml/1½ pints/3¾ cups
salt and freshly ground black pepper	
frozen peas	100 g/4 oz
fresh or frozen coriander (cilantro)	45 ml/3 tbsp
toasted unsalted almonds	100 g/4 oz/1 cup, roughly chopped
naan breads	to serve

1 Heat the oil in a large frying pan, add the onions and fry for 5 minutes until golden. Transfer to a plate with a slotted spoon leaving as much oil as possible behind in the pan.

2 Cut each chicken breast into three large chunks. Add to the frying pan and cook for 2 minutes until just beginning to turn opaque, then stir in the balti paste and cook for 30 seconds, stirring all the time.

3 Stir in the quinoa and cook for a further 30 seconds, then turn off the heat and stir in the tomatoes and stock. Season with salt and pepper.

4 Tip the mixture into a casserole dish (Dutch oven), making sure the dish fits in the halogen oven with a gap of at least 2.5 cm/1 in between it and the oven wall so the hot air can circulate). Cover with a lid or foil and cook on the low rack in the halogen oven at 190°C/375°F for 30 minutes.

5 Stir in the peas and coriander and cook for a further 3–4 minutes or until the chicken and quinoa are tender and cooked through. Scatter the toasted almonds over the balti.

6 If liked, the naan breads can be warmed in the halogen oven for a minute or two before serving.

turkey and leek cobbler pie

This tasty pie has a soft scone topping. The mixture is spooned on top, rather than the more usual rolling and cutting.

SERVES 4
READY IN **1 HOUR**

medium leeks	2, sliced
celery sticks	3, sliced
sunflower oil	15 ml/1 tbsp
unsalted (sweet) butter	15 g/½ oz/1 tbsp
plain (all-purpose) flour	15 ml/1 tbsp
double (heavy) cream or crème fraîche	75 ml/5 tbsp
hot chicken stock	250 ml/8 fl oz/1 cup
diced turkey breast	400 g/14 oz
dried mixed herbs	2.5 ml/½ tsp
salt and freshly ground black pepper	
For the cobbler topping:	
self-raising flour	150 g/5 oz/1¼ cups
butter	75 g/3 oz/generous ⅓ cup
milk	75 ml/5 tbsp
a green vegetable	to serve

1 Put the leeks and celery in a heatproof oven dish at least 7.5 cm/3 in deep. Drizzle with the oil and dot all over with the butter. Put on the low rack and cook at 250°C/500°F for 5 minutes or until the butter has melted.

2 Stir to coat the vegetables in the oil and butter, then cook for 10 minutes or until softened and beginning to colour.

3 Remove the dish from the oven, sprinkle the flour over and stir in, then gradually stir in the cream or crème fraîche, followed by the stock. Stir in the turkey breast, herbs, salt and pepper. Return to the oven, lower the temperature to 200°C/400°F and cook for 10 minutes while making the cobbler topping.

4 Put the flour in a bowl with a little salt and pepper. Cut the butter into small cubes, then rub into the flour until the mixture resembles breadcrumbs. Sprinkle the milk over and stir until the mixture just sticks together.

5 Top the turkey mixture with rounded tablespoonfuls of the cobbler dough, leaving spaces between each to allow them to rise and spread.

6 Cook for about 15 minutes or until the topping is well browned and cooked and the turkey and vegetables are tender.

7 Serve with a green vegetable.

salmon with ratatouille

Onions, courgettes, aubergines and peppers combine in a herby tomato sauce to make a delicious ratatouille.

SERVES 4
READY IN 1–1¼ HOURS

salmon fillets	4
salt and freshly ground black pepper	
olive oil	60 ml/4 tbsp
red onions	2, chopped
courgettes (zucchini)	2, diced
aubergine (eggplant)	1, diced
red (bell) pepper	1, diced
can of chopped tomatoes	400 g/14 oz/large
white wine or vegetable stock	100 ml/3½ fl oz/scant ½ cup
caster (superfine) sugar	a pinch
dried mixed herbs	2.5 ml/½ tsp
crusty french or italian bread or pasta	to serve

1 Season the salmon with salt and pepper and set aside. Put 30 ml/2 tbsp of the oil in a roasting tin and put on the low rack of the halogen oven. Heat to 200°C/400°F for 2–3 minutes.

2 Add the onions to the roasting tin and stir to coat in the oil, then cook for 5 minutes. Toss the courgettes and aubergine in the remaining oil, add to the tin and stir well. Cook for a further 10 minutes, stirring half-way through cooking to ensure even browning.

3 Add the diced pepper, tomatoes, wine or stock, sugar and herbs and stir well. Cook for 20 minutes, stirring once or twice, until the sauce has thickened a little and the vegetables are soft.

4 Place the salmon skin-side up on top of the sauce. Cook for a further 8 minutes or until the salmon is cooked through.

5 Serve with crusty French or Italian bread or pasta.

luxury
fish pie

Peas and sweetcorn are added to fresh or
smoked haddock and prawns, so there's no
need to cook any other vegetables.

SERVES 4
READY IN **50 MINUTES**

fresh or smoked **haddock fillet**	450 g/1 lb, skinned
shelled raw prawns **(shrimp)**	225 g/8 oz, halved if large
cornflour (cornstarch)	30 ml/2 tbsp
canned or frozen **sweetcorn**	100 g/4 oz
frozen peas	100 g/4 oz
packet of full-fat cream **cheese or cream cheese** **with garlic and herbs**	200 g/7 oz
milk	150 ml/¼ pint/⅔ cup
salt and freshly ground **black pepper**	
cold mashed potato	900 g/2 lb
or packets of ready-made **mashed potato**	2 x 400 g/14 oz

1 Cut the haddock into bite-sized pieces and place in a bowl with the prawns. Sprinkle the cornflour over and toss to coat. Add the sweetcorn and peas.

2 Blend together the cream cheese and milk and a little salt and pepper. Pour over the fish and vegetables (this mixture will be very thick but will be thinned with the cooking juices from the fish) and gently mix together. Spoon into an ovenproof dish (Dutch oven) – don't use a very deep dish or the fish won't cook through.

3 Give the mashed potato a brief stir to soften, then spoon on top of the fish mixture in an even layer.

4 Cook on the low rack at 175°C/340°F in the halogen oven for 30–35 minutes or until the fish and prawns are cooked and the potato topping is well browned. If the top starts to over-brown, cover with foil.

vegetable moussaka

Aubergine combined with other vegetables and layered with Feta cheese and passata. A yoghurt topping adds a flourish.

SERVES 4
READY IN 1¼ HOURS

V

potatoes	350 g/12 oz, cut into 2 cm/¾ in slices
salt and freshly ground black pepper	
onion	1, finely sliced
aubergine (eggplant)	1, cut into 2cm/¾ in slices
olive oil	45 ml/3 tbsp
garlic clove	1, finely chopped
passata (sieved tomatoes)	250 ml/8 fl oz/1 cup
dried Mediterranean or mixed herbs	5 ml/1 tsp
feta cheese	175 g/6 oz, crumbled
eggs	3, lightly beaten
plain yoghurt	250 ml/8 fl oz/1 cup
grated parmesan or mature cheddar cheese	25 g/1 oz/¼ cup
freshly grated nutmeg	a pinch
crusty bread and salad	to serve

1 Put the potato slices in a large pan and pour in just enough boiling water to cover. Add a pinch of salt, bring back to the boil and cook for 3 minutes. Add the onion and aubergine. Bring back to the boil and cook for a further 3–4 minutes until almost tender. Drain in a colander.

2 Tip the vegetables back into the pan, then drizzle with the oil. Mix together to coat the vegetables in oil, then tip on to a baking (cookie) sheet or tin that fits in the halogen oven (there will be quite a lot of vegetables for the pan, so spread them out as best as you can).

3 Roast on a low rack in the halogen oven at 200°C/400°F for 20 minutes, turning the vegetables two or three time during cooking so that they brown evenly and adding the garlic for the last 5 minutes of cooking.

4 Tip the vegetables back into the pan and add the passata, herbs, Feta and a good grinding of black pepper. Gently stir everything together, then transfer to a casserole (Dutch oven) or lasagne dish that fits in the halogen oven with a space of at least 2.5 cm/1 in between the dish and the oven wall.

5 Mix together the eggs, yoghurt, cheese and nutmeg and pour over the vegetables. Cover the dish with a lid or foil and cook on the low rack at 200°C/400°F for 25 minutes, removing the lid or foil for the last 5 minutes to allow the top to brown.

6 Serve with crusty bread and salad.

cheese and tomato filled aubergines

This impressive-looking Greek-inspired dish serves two as a healthy mid-week meal, or four as a starter or light lunch.

SERVES 2 OR 4
READY IN 50 MINUTES

small aubergines (eggplants)	2, about 15 cm/6 in long
sunflower oil	15 ml/1 tbsp
small red onion	1, finely chopped
garlic cloves,	2, crushed
or garlic purée (paste)	10 ml/2 tsp
tomatoes	2, chopped
chopped fresh or frozen parsley	30 ml/2 tbsp
dried oregano or thyme	1.5 ml/¼ tsp
salt and freshly ground black pepper	
cheddar or red leicestershire cheese	75 g/3 oz, grated
focaccia bread and salad	to serve

1 Without trimming the ends of the aubergines, cut them in half lengthways, then scoop out the flesh to leave a shell about 1 cm/½ in thick.

2 Put the aubergine shells on a baking tray and lightly brush the insides with the oil. Cook on the low rack in the halogen oven at 250°C/500°F for 5 minutes.

3 Meanwhile, finely chop the scooped-out aubergine flesh and put in a bowl with the onion, garlic, tomatoes and herbs. Season with salt and pepper and mix well.

4 Fill the aubergine shells with the stuffing, then return to the halogen oven and cook at 190°C/375°F for 20 minutes or until tender and cooked.

5 Sprinkle the cheese over and cook for a further 4–5 minutes or until the cheese is melted and bubbling.

6 Serve with foccacia and a mixed salad.

through the door and on the table in 30 minutes – using extras

Here you'll find the answer to that everyday dilemma – what to serve for supper that can be prepared and cooked in minutes but is both healthy and guaranteed to get the taste buds tingling.

There are already lots of quick and easy meals in the chapter on using just the basic oven, but in the next few pages you'll discover plenty more meals that take advantage of the extras you can get for your halogen oven, including perforated steamer trays and extender rings. Try 'Oriental beef with sesame noodles', 'Creamy pork and pears' or 'Cherry tomato and cheese tart'. Amazingly, all these dishes can be prepared in around half an hour or even a little less.

oriental beef with sesame noodles

Similar flavours to a classic stir-fry, but much healthier as this uses very little oil. Adding rocket at the end adds a peppery freshness.

SERVES 4
READY IN **30 MINUTES**

spring onions (scallions)	2, thinly sliced
red chilli,	1, seeded and finely chopped
or chilli purée (paste)	5 ml/1 tsp
garlic clove,	1, crushed
or garlic purée (paste)	5 ml/1 tsp
dark soy sauce	30 ml/2 tbsp
oyster sauce	15 ml/1 tbsp
balsamic vinegar	15 ml/1 tbsp
lean rump steak	350 g/12 oz, cut into thin strips
packet of ready-cooked rice noodles	300 g/11 oz
boiling stock or water	45 ml/3 tbsp
toasted sesame seeds	15 ml/1 tbsp
large red or yellow (bell) pepper	1, seeded and thinly sliced
celery stalks	4, thinly sliced
sunflower oil	10 ml/2 tsp
sesame oil, or extra sunflower oil	5 ml/1 tsp
rocket (arugula) leaves	25 g/1 oz

1 Put the low rack in the halogen oven, then preheat it to 250°C/500°F. Mix the spring onions, chilli, garlic, soy sauce, oyster sauce and balsamic vinegar in a bowl. Add the steak and stir until well coated. Set aside for a few minutes while preparing the vegetables and noodles.

2 Rinse out a heatproof dish with very hot water. Add the noodles and sprinkle the stock or water over, then the sesame seeds. Cover tightly with foil and place on the low rack. Add the high rack to the oven.

3 Toss the sliced pepper and celery in the oils on a baking tray and spread out evenly. Place on the high rack and cook for 6–8 minutes, stirring half-way through cooking, until lightly browned in places.

4 Scatter the beef over the vegetables and continue cooking for 3–4 minutes or until the beef is browned.

5 Turn off the oven, scatter the rocket over the beef, replace the oven lid and leave to wilt for a minute.

6 Transfer the noodles to warmed plates. Mix together the vegetables, beef and rocket and spoon on top. Serve straight away.

creamy pork and pears

Pork and pears are classic food partners. Choose firm but just ripe pears; they should just yield to pressure when lightly pressed.

SERVES 4
READY IN **30 MINUTES**

firm ripe pears	2, cored and cut into wedges
oil	a little for greasing
pork loin steaks	4, trimmed
dry cider	100 ml/3½ fl oz/generous ⅓ cup
crème fraîche	150 ml/¼ pint/⅔ cup
salt and freshly ground black pepper	
cooked new potatoes	400 g/14 oz, halved
a green vegetable	to serve

1 Put the pear wedges on a lightly oiled baking tray on the lower rack of the halogen oven. Lightly oil the upper rack and place the pork steaks on it. Cook the steaks for 2–3 minutes on each side until lightly browned, and the pears for 5 minutes at 200°C/400°F. Set aside.

2 While the pears and pork are cooking, heat the cider in a pan on the hob until it is steaming hot. Whisk in the crème fraîche and season with salt and pepper, then stir in the new potatoes and pear wedges. Heat again until the sauce starts to bubble.

3 Tip into an ovenproof casserole dish (Dutch oven) that fits in the halogen oven with a gap of at least 2.5 cm/ 1 in between the dish and the oven wall so the hot air can circulate.

4 Place the pork steaks on top and return to the low rack of the halogen oven for 6–8 minutes or until the pork is cooked through and the sauce is bubbling.

5 Serve with a green vegetable such as broccoli or beans.

honey and mustard gammon with corn

Gammon steaks glazed with mustard and honey are served with cheesy mashed potatoes mixed with sweetcorn.

SERVES 4
READY IN **30 MINUTES**

packets of mashed potato	2 x 400 g/14 oz
can of sweetcorn with peppers	200 g/7 oz/small, drained
mature cheddar cheese	75 g/3 oz, grated
dried chilli flakes	a large pinch
gammon steaks, each 200–250g (7–8 oz)	4, trimmed
wholegrain mustard	20 ml/4 tsp
clear honey	30 ml/2 tbsp
lemon juice	10 ml/2 tsp
freshly ground black pepper	

1 Tip the mashed potato into a bowl and stir in the sweetcorn, cheese and chilli flakes. Spoon into a shallow heatproof dish and fork the surface. Place on the low rack in the halogen oven. Turn on the oven to 200°C/400°F and cook for 3–4 minutes while preparing the steaks.

2 Put the steaks on a non-stick baking tray. Mix together the mustard, honey, lemon juice and a little black pepper and brush half over one side of the steaks.

3 Add the high rack and the extender ring to the halogen oven. Put the gammon steaks on the high rack and cook for 5 minutes. Turn them over and brush with the remaining mustard mixture.

4 Cook for a further 5 minutes or until the steaks are cooked through.

5 Serve with the corn, cheese and chilli mash.

simple chicken satay

Good food – but simple and speedy. If your metal skewers won't fit in the halogen oven, use soaked wooden ones, trimmed to fit.

SERVES 4
READY IN **30 MINUTES**

carton of creamed coconut	250 g/9 oz
crunchy peanut butter	90 ml/6 tbsp
worcestershire sauce	5 ml/1 tsp
lemon juice	30 ml/2 tbsp
boneless, skinless chicken breasts	4, cut into chunks
naan breads	4
cucumber	¼, thinly sliced
large carrot	1, coarsely grated
salted peanuts	25 g/1 oz/¼ cup, roughly chopped

1 Stir together the creamed coconut, peanut butter, Worcestershire sauce and 15 ml/1 tbsp of the lemon juice (you may need to warm this mixture in a pan on the hob if the coconut cream has solidified).

2 Spoon half the sauce into a bowl, add the chicken and stir to coat. Thread on to metal skewers, then place on a baking tray.

3 Wrap the naan breads tightly in foil and place on the low rack in the halogen oven, then position the high rack in the oven and add the chicken skewers.

4 Cook at 200°C/400°F for 8–10 minutes until lightly browned and cooked through, turning the chicken half-way through the cooking time.

5 Meanwhile, mix together the cucumber and carrot. Stir the remaining 15 ml/1 tbsp of lemon juice into the reserved satay sauce and warm gently on the hob.

6 Unwrap the naan breads and put on plates. Top each with some of the carrot and cucumber mix, then top with a chicken skewer (remove the meat from the skewer first, if you like). Drizzle the sauce over and scatter with the chopped peanuts.

tarragon chicken with mushrooms

Tarragon is *the* herb for chicken. It retains much of its flavour when dried, so it makes a good substitute if don't have fresh.

SERVES 4
READY IN **30 MINUTES**

baby button mushrooms	100 g/4 oz
chicken stock	45 ml/3 tbsp
celery sticks	4, thinly sliced
garlic clove,	1, crushed
or garlic purée (paste)	5 ml/1 tsp
sprigs of fresh tarragon,	4
or dried tarragon	2.5 ml/½ tsp
dry white wine	45 ml/3 tbsp
salt and freshly ground black pepper	
boneless, skinless chicken breasts	4
olive oil	15 ml/1 tbsp
sachets of ready-cooked long-grain rice,	2 x 250 g/9 oz
or cooked rice	500 g/18 oz
hot chicken stock or water	30 ml/2 tbsp
double (heavy) cream (optional)	15 ml/1 tbsp

1 Put the mushrooms and stock in a heatproof dish and put on the low rack in the halogen oven. Add the high rack.

2 Put the celery, garlic and tarragon in a deep heatproof dish. Spoon the wine over, season with salt and pepper and mix together. Place the chicken breasts on top and brush with the oil. Put on the high rack and add the extender ring.

3 Cook at 250°C/500°F for 5 minutes or until the chicken is beginning to brown, then turn the chicken over and cook for a further 5 minutes. Remove the chicken and set aside.

4 Tip the mushrooms and liquid into the dish with the celery and stir together. Put the rice in a dish and sprinkle the stock or water over. Cover tightly with pierced foil and place on the low rack. Put the dish of vegetables on the high rack.

5 Cook for 5–6 minutes or until the vegetables are just tender, turning them if they start to brown too much, then arrange the chicken on top again and cook for a further 6–7 minutes or until cooked through and tender.

6 Stir the cream, if using, into the vegetable juices, then serve the chicken and vegetables on a bed of the rice with the sauce spooned over.

sticky chicken wings with herby bread

Cheap and cheerful chicken wings take on a star role when coated in a rich sticky glaze and served with crunchy herb bread.

SERVES 4
READY IN **30 MINUTES**

thick honey	30 ml/2 tbsp
tomato ketchup (catsup)	30 ml/2 tbsp
dijon mustard	15 ml/1 tbsp
wine vinegar	15 ml/1 tbsp
soy sauce	10 ml/2 tsp
sunflower oil	10 ml/2 tsp
salt and freshly ground black pepper	
chicken wings	16
For the herby bread:	
short baguette, approx 18 cm/7 in long	1
butter, softened	50 g/2 oz/¼ cup
chopped fresh or frozen herbs such as parsley or mixed herbs	30 ml/2 tbsp
a mixed salad or coleslaw	to serve

1 Put the honey, ketchup, mustard, vinegar, soy sauce, oil and a pinch of salt and pepper in a large bowl. Stir together, then add the chicken wings and mix to coat in the sauce. Leave to marinate while preparing the herby bread.

2 If necessary, trim the ends off the baguette so that it will fit in the halogen oven. Make 2.5 cm/1 in slices into the bread, but do not go all the way through the bottom crust.

3 Mix together the butter, herbs and a little salt and pepper. Spread a teaspoonful or two of the butter mixture between each slice. Wrap in foil and put on the low rack in the halogen oven. Position the high rack on top, then turn on the oven to 250°C/500°F.

4 Transfer the coated chicken wings to a baking tray and place on the high rack. Cook for 15–20 minutes or until thoroughly cooked, turning over half-way through the cooking time and moving around on the baking tray so they brown evenly.

5 Remove the chicken wings and high rack. Open up the foil on the garlic bread and cook for 2–3 minutes until browned while serving up the wings.

6 Serve with a mixed salad or coleslaw.

turkey and apple pittas

These home-made turkey burgers are healthily lean and full of flavour. Juice from the grated apple keeps them moist.

SERVES 4
READY IN **30 MINUTES**

minced (ground) turkey	500 g/18 oz
eating (dessert) apple	1, cored, peeled and grated
dried mixed herbs	a pinch
dried chilli flakes or powder	a pinch
salt and freshly ground black pepper	
plain (all-purpose) flour	15 ml/1 tbsp
large pitta breads	4
ready-made tzatziki or mayonnaise, sliced tomatoes and salad leaves	to serve

1 Put the turkey, apple, herbs and chilli flakes in a bowl and season with salt and pepper. Mix together, then shape into four balls.

2 Lightly coat the balls in the flour, then shape into oval patties each about 2.5 cm/1 in thick. Place on a lightly greased baking tray.

3 Put both the low and high racks in the halogen oven. Put the patties on the high rack and cook at 250°C/500°F for about 10 minutes or until well browned on top.

4 Wrap the pittas tightly in foil and put on the low rack. Turn the patties over and continue cooking on the high rack for 7–8 minutes or until the second side is browned and the meat is cooked right through. (If necessary, reduce the temperature to 175°C/340°F and cook for a few more minutes).

5 Split open the pittas and place the patties inside with some tzatziki or mayonnaise, sliced tomatoes and salad leaves. Serve straight away.

roasted vegetables with chick peas

This dish is suitable for vegans as well as vegetarians. Like other pulses, chick peas are a useful source of protein.

SERVES 4
READY IN **30 MINUTES**

V

For the roasted vegetables:

small red onions	6, cut into wedges
red (bell) pepper	1, seeded and thickly sliced
yellow pepper	1, seeded and thickly sliced
plum tomatoes	4, cut into chunks
olive oil	30 ml/2 tbsp
harissa paste	5 ml/1 tsp
caster (superfine) sugar	a pinch
salt and freshly ground black pepper	

For the chick pea bulghar:

bulghar (cracked wheat)	225 g/8 oz/2 cups
bay leaf	1
lemon zest (optional)	a strip
boiling vegetable stock or water	300 ml/½ pint/1¼ cups
can of chick peas (garbanzos)	400 g/14 oz/large
olive oil	5 ml/1 tsp
lemon juice	30 ml/2 tbsp

1 Place both the low and high racks and the extender ring in the halogen oven.

2 To make the roasted vegetables, place the onions, peppers and tomatoes in a roasting tray. Blend together the oil, harissa paste, sugar and salt and pepper, drizzle over the vegetables and toss to mix. Place on the high rack and cook at 250°C/500°F for 5–6 minutes.

3 Meanwhile, to make the bulghar, put the bulghar in a heatproof dish, add the bay leaf and lemon zest, if using, and pour the stock or water over. Drain the chick peas through a sieve (strainer) and pour over some boiling water to rinse and heat them through. Stir into the bulghar. Cover tightly with foil.

4 Take the vegetables out of the halogen oven and move them around on the tray. Put the bulghar wheat on the low rack, then the vegetables back on the top rack. Cook for 20 minutes or until tender, turning the vegetables once or twice during cooking so that they brown evenly.

5 Whisk together the oil and lemon juice with a little salt and pepper. Stir into the bulghar wheat, then spoon on to warmed plates. Serve topped with the roasted vegetables.

cherry tomato and cheese tart

Although green pesto is more well known, do try red pesto, which contains sun-dried tomatoes. It's also an excellent pizza topping.

SERVES 4
READY IN **30 MINUTES**

ready-rolled puff pastry (paste)	1 x 200 g/7 oz sheet
red pesto	30 ml/2 tbsp
feta cheese	75 g/3 oz/¾ cup, crumbled
red and yellow cherry tomatoes	200 g/7 oz, halved
mozzarella cheese	75 g/3 oz/¾ cup, coarsely grated or diced
baby leaf salad or rocket (arugula) leaves	to serve

1 Remove the pastry from the fridge and leave it at at room temperature for at least a minute or two (preferably 10–15 minutes as this will prevent it cracking as you unroll it) while preparing the other ingredients. Line a round halogen oven crisping/steaming tray measuring 23 cm/9 in across the base with a round of baking parchment. Place the high rack in the oven and preheat to 200°C/400°F.

2 Unroll the pastry and, using a plate as a guide, cut out a round slightly smaller than 23 cm/9 in. Place in the lined steaming tray and prick all over with a fork. Cook for 5–6 minutes or until puffy and lightly browned.

3 Place a round baking tray the same size as the steaming tray over the pastry, then invert the pastry, uncooked-side up, on to the baking tray and carefully peel away the baking parchment.

4 Spread the red pesto over the pastry in an even layer to about 1 cm/½ in from the edge of the pastry to form a border. Scatter with the Feta, then arrange the tomatoes, cut-side up, on top. Scatter with the Mozzarella.

5 Bake for a further 7–8 minutes or until the pastry is puffed up and both the pastry and cheese are browned.

6 Serve hot with a baby leaf salad or rocket leaves.

grilled vegetable bake

This quick and easy dish uses a bag of frozen grilled Mediterranean vegetables, so involves little preparation.

SERVES 4
READY IN 30 MINUTES

V

packet of frozen grilled mediterranean vegetables	450 g/ 1 lb, preferably thawed
dijon mustard	2.5 ml/½ tsp
ground almonds	60 ml/4 tbsp
fresh white breadcrumbs	30 ml/2 tbsp
milk	300 ml/½ pint/1¼ cups
eggs	3
salt and freshly ground black pepper	
gruyère (swiss) cheese	100 g/4 oz/1 cup, grated
ciabatta or foccacia bread	to serve

1 Spread out the vegetables in an ovenproof dish that fits in the halogen oven with a gap of at least 2.5 cm/1 in between the dish and the oven wall so the hot air can circulate.

2 Stir together the mustard, almonds, breadcrumbs and a little of the milk in a heatproof jug or bowl (check it is not too tall to fit in the halogen oven), then stir in the rest of the milk. Cover tightly with foil and place in the bottom of the halogen oven.

3 Place the high rack over the bowl or jug. Put the vegetables on the high rack and cook at 250°C/500°F for 4–5 minutes to warm the vegetables and the milk mixture.

4 Meanwhile, whisk the eggs with a little salt and pepper. Remove the vegetables and milk and the high rack from the halogen oven. Reduce the temperature to 175°C/340°F.

5 Add the eggs to the jug of warmed milk and stir well. Scatter the cheese evenly over the vegetables, then pour the egg and milk mixture over. Cook on the low rack for 20 minutes or until the mixture is lightly set (check this by pushing a thin knife or skewer into the middle – it should feel hot and there should be little liquid).

6 Serve hot with ciabatta or focaccia bread.

meals from your oven using extra accessories

Accessories packs that contain extra racks, steamer pans, baking trays and even skewers expand the repertoire of meals that can be cooked in your halogen oven, as this chapter illustrates. As well as all-in-one dishes, you can now cook accompaniments separately.

Try 'Apricot and pine nut pork with lemon rice' or a roast chicken with all the vegetables – perfect for Sunday lunch – or perhaps 'Glamorgan brunch', a fabulous brunch with home-made vegetarian sausages and roasted mushrooms and tomatoes. Some of the meals here may be a little more time-consuming but none is complicated.

easy beef stroganoff

Lean steak and whole baby button mushrooms give this dish a feeling of real luxury.

SERVES 4
READY IN **1¾–2 HOURS**

butter, preferably unsalted (sweet)	25 g/1 oz/2 tbsp
onion	1, very thinly sliced
baby button mushrooms	225g/8 oz, halved
lean rump steak	550 g/1½ lb, trimmed and cut into 1 cm/½ in strips
paprika	15 ml/1 tbsp
can of cream of mushroom soup	400 g/14 oz/large
worcestershire sauce	15 ml/1 tbsp
salt and freshly ground pepper	
sachets of ready-cooked long-grain rice	2 x 250 g/9 oz
cold water or stock	30 ml/2 tbsp
soured cream or crème fraîche	30 ml/2 tbsp
chopped fresh or frozen parsley	30 ml/2 tbsp
a green vegetable	to serve

1 Put the butter on a baking tray and heat on the high rack in the halogen cooker at 100°C/200°F for 2–3 minutes or until melted.

2 Add the onion and stir to coat, then turn up the heat to 200°C/400°F and cook for 5 minutes, stirring half-way through the cooking time. Add the mushrooms, stir and cook for 2–3 minutes.

3 Add the beef and stir well. Cook for a further 10 minutes, stirring half-way through the cooking time to brown the beef evenly.

4 Tip the mixture into a casserole dish (Dutch oven), making sure that there is a gap of at least 2.5 cm/1 in between the dish and the oven wall so the hot air can circulate. Sprinkle the paprika over, then stir in, followed by the soup and Worcestershire sauce. Season with salt and pepper.

5 Put the rice in a dish and sprinkle the water or stock over. Stir to break up any large clumps of rice, then cover tightly with foil and place on the low rack. Cover the beef mixture with pierced foil and return to the high rack. Add the extender ring and cook for 30–40 minutes or until the beef and vegetables are very tender.

6 Stir the soured cream or crème fraîche and parsley into the beef.

7 Serve with the rice and a green vegetable.

lamb tikka kebabs

A marinade of yoghurt and lemon together with aromatic spices is the key to success for these tender and juicy kebabs.

SERVES 4
READY IN **30–40 MINUTES, PLUS MARINATING**

For the kebabs:

natural yoghurt	150 ml/¼ pint/⅔ cup
lemon juice	15 ml/1 tbsp
sunflower oil, plus extra for greasing	5 ml/1 tsp
garlic clove, or garlic purée (paste)	1, crushed 5 ml/1 tsp
ground coriander	5 ml/1 tsp
garam masala	5 ml/1 tsp
mild chilli powder	5 ml/1 tsp
ground turmeric	2.5 ml/½ tsp
salt	a pinch
lean lamb such as tenderloin	450 g/1 lb, cut into 2.5 cm/1 in pieces
naan breads or chappatis	4

For the cucumber and tomato raita:

cucumber	5 cm/2 in piece, finely chopped
baby plum tomatoes	150 g/5 oz, quartered
red wine vinegar	5 ml/1 tsp
sunflower oil	10 ml/2 tsp
salt and freshly ground black pepper	
natural yoghurt	30 ml/2 tbsp
chopped fresh or frozen coriander (cilantro) or mint	30 ml/2 tbsp

1 To make the kebabs, soak eight wooden skewers in cold water for several hours (this prevents them burning during cooking), making sure that they will fit in the halogen oven (if not, you may need to trim the ends).

2 Put the yoghurt, lemon juice, oil, garlic, spices and salt in a bowl and mix together. Add the lamb and stir well to coat. Cover and leave to marinate in the fridge for 3–4 hours.

3 Wrap the naan breads or chappatis in foil and place on the low rack. Thread the lamb on to the soaked skewers and place them on a lightly oiled baking tray on the upper rack in the halogen oven.

4 Cook at 225°C/437°F for about 15 minutes, turning the kebabs occasionally so that they brown and cook evenly.

5 While the kebabs are cooking, to make the raita put the cucumber and tomatoes in a bowl and sprinkle the vinegar and oil over. Season with salt and pepper and mix together. Add the yoghurt and herbs and mix again.

6 Serve the raita with the kebabs and hot naan breads or chappatis.

lamb shanks with red wine

Flavoursome lamb shanks make the perfect individual portion. Braising with a dash of wine adds depth and a rich colour.

SERVES 4
READY IN **2¼–2½ HOURS**

lamb shanks	4
olive oil	45 ml/3 tbsp
onion	1, chopped
celery sticks	2, chopped
medium leek	1, chopped
garlic cloves,	2, crushed
or garlic purée (paste)	10 ml/2 tsp
new potatoes	350 g/12 oz, quartered
red wine	150 ml/¼ pint/⅔ cup
dried rosemary or mixed herbs	5 ml/1 tsp
boiling lamb or vegetable stock	300 ml/½ pint/1¼ cups
salt and freshly ground black pepper	
a green vegetable	to serve

1 Put the lamb shanks on a baking tray and rub all over with 15 ml/1 tbsp of the oil. Cook on the low rack in the halogen oven at 250°C/500°F for 10 minutes, turning several times, until well-browned all over.

2 Transfer the lamb shanks to a casserole dish (Dutch oven), leaving no more than 30 ml/2 tbsp of fat and juices behind on the tray (make sure there is a gap of at least 2.5 cm/1 in between the dish and the oven wall so the hot air can circulate).

3 Put the casserole dish on the low rack and add the high rack and extender ring. Add the onion to the fat in the baking tray and stir to coat. Cook for 5 minutes until beginning to brown.

4 Add the celery, leek, garlic and potatoes and stir to coat. Reduce the temperature to 180°C/350°F and cook for 10 minutes, stirring half-way through the cooking time.

5 Add the vegetables to the casserole dish, tucking them between the lamb shanks, and pour the red wine over. Stir the herbs into the stock and season with salt and pepper, then pour into the casserole dish.

6 Cover with a lid or pierced foil and cook for 1¼–1½ hours or until the meat is very tender and almost falling off the bone. (If the lamb shanks aren't completely submerged in the liquid, turn them half-way through the cooking time.)

7 Serve with a green vegetable.

apricot and pine nut pork with lemon rice

The sharp sweetness of apricots is the perfect match for pork. Short pork loins will fit in the halogen oven easier than long ones.

 SERVES 4
READY IN **1 HOUR**

pork tenderloin (2 whole fillets)	450 g/1 lb, trimmed
toasted pine nuts	25 g/1 oz/¼ cup
ready-to-eat dried apricots	25 g/1 oz
salt and freshly ground black pepper	
butter	25 g/1 oz/2 tbsp
olive oil	30 ml/2 tbsp
easy-cook rice	175 g/6 oz/⅔ cup
lemon	1, finely grated zest only
boiling vegetable or chicken stock	450 ml/¾ pint/2 cups
thin green beans	150 g/5 oz
clear honey	5 ml/1 tsp

1 Make a pocket in each pork fillet by cutting lengthways about three-quarters of the way through. Open up the fillets and place on a board.

2 Roughly chop the pine nuts, then chop the apricots into pieces of a similar size. Season the pork with salt and pepper, sprinkle the nuts and apricots over, then dot with the butter. Fold the tenderloins back over the filling to enclose it, then wrap each tightly in clingfilm (plastic wrap) and twist the ends.

3 Use 15 ml/1 tbsp of the oil to grease the inside of a casserole (Dutch oven) or baking dish. Add the rice and sprinkle the lemon zest and a little salt and pepper over. Pour the stock over, then cover with a lid or foil and place on the low rack of the halogen oven. Cook at 200°C/400°F for 15 minutes.

4 Meanwhile, trim the beans and half widthways. Stir into the rice and re-cover. Cook for 10 minutes. Position the high rack and extender ring in the halogen oven.

5 Put the pork in a second casserole dish and pour over enough boiling water to cover. Cover the dish with a lid or foil and place on the high rack. Cook for 15 minutes or until the pork is almost cooked through.

6 Remove the pork from the oven and take off the clingfilm. Pat the pork dry with kitchen paper (paper towels) and put on a baking tray. Mix together the remaining oil and the honey and brush all over the pork. Cook for 3–4 minutes until lightly browned, then turn over and cook the other side for 3–4 minutes.

7 Remove the pork from the oven, cover with foil and leave to rest for 2–3 minutes. Meanwhile, check the rice. It should be cooked but if not cook for a few more minutes or until the rice and beans are tender and all the stock has been absorbed. Cut the pork into slices and serve with the rice.

roast loin of pork with sultana stuffing

Sultanas are an unusual ingredient for a savoury stuffing, but combined with orange they add a unique flavour to the pork.

SERVES 4
READY IN **1¼ HOURS**

sultanas (golden raisins)	75 g/3 oz/½ cup
orange	1, grated zest and juice only
sunflower oil	60 ml/4 tbsp
roughly chopped fresh or frozen parsley	30 ml/2 tbsp
dried rosemary or mixed herbs	2.5 ml/½ tsp
salt and freshly ground black pepper	
potatoes	450 g/1 lb, cut into large chunks
parsnips	2, cut into large chunks
carrots	2, cut into large chunks
medium-sized pork joint with rind	1, about 10 cm/4 in thick, about 750 g/1¾ lb

1 Put the sultanas in a small bowl with the orange zest and juice. Cover with clingfilm (plastic wrap), put in the fridge and leave to soak for at least 4 hours.

2 Tip the contents of the bowl into a food processor, add 30 ml/2 tbsp of the oil and the parsley and process until finely chopped. Add the dried herbs, a little salt and pepper and process for a few more seconds.

3 Put the potatoes, parsnips and carrots in a pan and pour over just enough boiling water to cover. Add a pinch of salt and bring to the boil. Simmer for 3 minutes, then drain. Drizzle 15 ml/1 tbsp of the oil over them and gently toss to coat. Tip on to a baking tray on the low rack.

4 Lay the pork skin-side up and use a sharp knife to score the rind crossways. Turn the meat over and split almost in half by slicing horizontally through the meat towards the fatty side. Open it up and spread the stuffing on the bottom half.

5 Tie the joint back into its original shape, then rub the skin liberally with the remaining oil and sprinkle with salt. Put the pork on the high rack, skin-side down, and add the extender ring. Cook at 250°C/500°F for 5 minutes; if necessary, use a couple of ovenproof ramekins (custard cups) to prop it up.

6 Turn the joint to skin-side up and cook for 7–10 minutes, moving it occasionally to brown the crackling evenly. Turn down the heat to 180°C/350°F and cook for a further 20 minutes, again moving occasionally. Check the meat is cooked through by piercing it with a skewer or sharp knife; the juices should run clear.

7 Allow the meat to rest in a warm place for 10 minutes. Remove the extender ring. Drain the vegetables, then tip on to the baking tray. Turn up the heat to 225°C/437°F and cook for 7–8 minutes, turning once, until crispy. Slice the pork and serve with the vegetables.

lemon and herb roast chicken

A firm family favourite, this is an almost unbelievably simple way to cook a Sunday roast – all in the halogen oven!

 SERVES 4
READY IN **1½ HOURS**

oven-ready chicken	1, about 1.5 kg/3 lb
salt and freshly ground black pepper	
lemon	1, halved
sprigs of fresh herbs such as thyme and rosemary (optional)	a few
sunflower oil	45 ml/3 tbsp
even-sized new potatoes	450 g/1 lb
carrots	4, cut into 7.5 cm/3 in lengths

1 Season the cavity of the chicken with salt and pepper, then add the lemon halves and fresh herbs. Rub the chicken all over with 30 ml/2 tbsp of the oil. Place the chicken, breast-side down, on the low rack.

2 Put the potatoes and carrots in the halogen oven bowl, drizzle with the remaining oil and toss to coat. Place the rack with the chicken in the oven.

3 Add the extender ring and cook at 200°C/400°F for 35 minutes or until well browned. If possible, baste occasionally with the juices using a bulb baster. Carefully turn the chicken over and cook for a further 30 minutes or until cooked through (the juices should run clear when the thigh is pierced).

4 Remove the extender ring, chicken and rack. Cover the chicken with foil to keep it warm and leave it to rest for 10–15 minutes.

5 Drain the vegetables and tip into the roasting tin. Increase the temperature to 250°C/500°F and cook on the low rack for a further 10–15 minutes or until they are tender and browned. Carve the chicken and serve with the vegetables. If liked, the juices can be skimmed of excess fat, strained and served as a gravy.

Handy tip

You could also prepare a packet of stuffing mix and cook it on the low rack, with the vegetables on the high rack with the extender ring, for the last 10–15 minutes of the cooking time. Quickly brown the stuffing (without the extender ring) for 2–3 minutes while serving up the vegetables.

pot roast chicken

This chicken remains moist and succulent in the halogen oven and the breast is basted with herby butter.

SERVES 4
READY IN **1 HOUR**

oven-ready chicken	1, about 1.5 kg/3 lb
butter	15 g/½ oz/1 tbsp, softened
chopped fresh parsley,	15 ml/1 tbsp
or dried mixed herbs	5 ml/1 tsp
salt and freshly ground black pepper	
potatoes	450 g/1 lb, cut into large chunks
carrots	4, halved widthways
celery sticks,	2, cut into 2.5 cm/1 in lengths
leeks	2, cut into 2.5 cm/1 in lengths
garlic clove	1, peeled
bay leaf	1
chicken stock cube	1

1 Put the chicken on a roasting tray on the low rack. Blend together the butter and herbs with a little salt and pepper. Carefully loosen the skin on the breast of the chicken and spread the herb butter underneath. Put the extender ring on the halogen oven and cook at 200°C/400°F for 10 minutes or until the skin is starting to brown.

2 Turn the chicken over and cook for a further 25 minutes or until the underneath of the chicken is browned.

3 While the chicken is cooking, put the potatoes, carrots, celery and leeks in a saucepan with the garlic and bay leaf. Pour over just enough boiling water to cover and simmer for 7–8 minutes. Lift out the vegetables with a slotted spoon.

4 Pour 250 ml/8 fl oz/1 cup of the cooking water into a jug. Crumble in the stock cube and stir until dissolved.

5 Remove the chicken and low rack from the oven (discard the fat and juices in the pan). Put the vegetables in the halogen oven bowl and pour the stock over. Place the chicken on top of the vegetables, breast-side up, and cook for a further 25 minutes.

6 Check that the meat is cooked through by piercing the thickest part of the thigh with a knife; the juices should run clear (cook for a little longer, if necessary). Leave the chicken to rest in a warm place. Meanwhile, skim the fat from the surface of the stock. Stir the vegetables and cook for a further 5–10 minutes without the extender ring until the stock is bubbling and the vegetables are tender.

7 Lower the heat to 150°C/300°F to keep the vegetables warm while you carve the chicken, then serve with the vegetables. Strain the chicken juices into a warmed jug and serve as gravy.

italian stuffed chicken

This Mediterranean-style chicken is fantastic for entertaining. You could substitute full-fat or 'light' soft cheese for the Mascarpone.

SERVES 4
READY IN **45 MINUTES**

For the stuffed chicken:

mascarpone cheese	100 g/4 oz/½ cup
chopped stoned (pitted) black olives	30 ml/2 tbsp
dried mixed herbs	2.5 ml/½ tsp
garlic clove,	1, crushed
or garlic purée (paste)	5 ml/1 tsp
skinless chicken breasts	4
olive oil	15 ml/1 tbsp, plus extra for greasing
firm ripe tomatoes	4
balsamic vinegar	5 ml/1 tsp

For the rosemary roast potatoes:

even-sized small new potatoes	350 g/12 oz, scrubbed
olive oil	15 ml/1 tbsp
dried rosemary	5 ml/1 tsp
salt	

1 To make the stuffed chicken, put the Mascarpone cheese in a bowl. Add the olives, herbs and garlic and mix well.

2 Cut a slit along the side of each chicken breast, then open it out into a pocket. Stuff each chicken breast with a quarter of the cheese mixture, then press the edges together to close the chicken around the filling. Place on a lightly oiled baking tray and arrange the tomato slices on top.

3 Whisk together the oil and balsamic vinegar and drizzle over the tomatoes. Put on the low rack in the halogen oven, then position the high rack and the extender ring.

4 To make the rosemary roast potatoes, toss the potatoes in a mixture of the oil, rosemary and a little salt. Place on a baking tray and put on the high rack.

5 Cook at 200°C/400°F for 15 minutes, turning the potatoes once or twice during cooking so that they brown evenly.

6 Switch the chicken to the high rack and the potatoes to the low rack. Cook for a further 5–10 minutes or until both are cooked and browned.

herby chicken thighs with potato cakes

The potato cakes are such a great way to turn plain mashed potato into something special that it's worth cooking extra.

 SERVES 4
READY IN **50 MINUTES**

chicken thighs	4, boned
salt and freshly ground black pepper	
olive oil	15 ml/1 tbsp
fresh or bottled lemon juice	5 ml/1 tsp
garlic clove,	1, crushed
or garlic purée (paste)	5 ml/1 tsp
chopped fresh or frozen parsley or coriander (cilantro)	30 ml/2 tbsp
plain (all-purpose) flour	30 ml/2 tbsp
spring onions (scallions)	4, finely chopped
cool mashed potato (leftovers or bought ready-mashed)	450 g/1 lb
white wine	60 ml/4 tbsp
a green vegetable, sweetcorn or a salad	to serve

1 Put the chicken thighs, flesh-side up, on a board and season generously with salt and pepper. Mix together 5 ml/1 tsp of the oil, the lemon juice, garlic and chopped herbs and divide between the thighs.

2 Roll up each chicken thigh tightly and place, seam-side down, in a shallow ovenproof dish (ideally just big enough to hold the chicken with very small gaps between each). Brush the skin with 5 ml/1 tsp of the oil. Set aside to allow the flavours to penetrate the chicken.

3 Meanwhile, stir the flour and spring onions into the mashed potatoes, seasoning with salt and pepper (if the mash isn't already seasoned). Shape into potato cakes about 5 cm/2 in thick and place on a non-stick baking tray. Lightly brush the tops with a little of the remaining oil.

4 Cook the potato cakes on the low rack in the halogen oven at 250°C/500°F for 10 minutes, turning once and brushing the uncooked side with oil, until lightly browned.

5 Reduce the temperature to 200°C/400°F and add the extender ring and the high rack to the halogen oven. Pour the wine into the dish with the chicken and cook for 15 minutes or until well-browned and cooked through (test by piercing with a fine knife or skewer – the juices should run clear).

6 Transfer the chicken to warmed plates and spoon the juices over.

7 Serve with the hot potato cakes and a green vegetable, sweetcorn or a side salad.

tandoori chicken with coriander naans

Home-made tandoori is a healthy alternative to takeaways or dining out and is simplified by using ready-made curry pastes.

SERVES 4
READY IN **35–40 MINUTES, PLUS MARINATING**

boneless chicken breasts	4
greek-style yoghurt	250 ml/8 fl oz/1 cup
sunflower oil	20 ml/1½ tbsp
ready-made tandoori paste,	15 ml/1 tbsp
or ground cumin, ground coriander, turmeric, mild chilli powder, paprika and salt	2.5 ml/½ tsp each
freshly ground black pepper	
butter	40 g/1½ oz/3 tbsp, softened
large garlic clove,	1, crushed
or garlic purée (paste)	5 ml/1 tsp
chopped fresh or frozen coriander (cilantro)	30 ml/2 tbsp
medium-sized naan breads	4
hot water	30 ml/2 tbsp
raita or a tomato salad	to serve

1 Cut deep slashes into the chicken at 2.5 cm/1 in intervals. Mix together the yoghurt, oil, curry paste or dry spices and black pepper in a bowl, then spoon and rub the marinade all over the chicken. Cover and chill for at least 1 hour, preferably for several hours or overnight.

2 Blend together the butter, garlic and coriander and spread thinly over one side of each naan bread. Place on the low rack in the halogen oven (it is fine if they overlap a little). Add the high rack to the oven.

3 Scrape a little, but not all, of the marinade from the chicken breasts back into the bowl and reserve. Place the chicken breasts on a non-stick baking tray and place on the high rack. Cook at 200°C/400°F for 5 minutes until lightly browned.

4 Meanwhile, stir the hot water into the reserved marinade. Turn the chicken over and spoon the marinade over. Cook for a further 6–8 minutes or until browned and cooked through.

5 Transfer the chicken to warmed plates and remove the high rack. Cook the naan breads for a further 2–3 minutes or until the butter has melted and is sizzling (you may need to switch them around, so that they cook evenly).

6 Serve with the chicken and some bought cucumber raita or a tomato salad (you could use the raita recipe on page 108).

spinach and ricotta cannelloni

If you want to make this a vegetarian meal, simply leave out the Parma ham or replace it with chopped red or yellow (bell) peppers.

 SERVES 4
READY IN **1 HOUR**

frozen spinach	225 g/8 oz, thawed
parma ham or lean bacon	50 g/2 oz, chopped
ricotta cheese	200 g/7 oz/scant 1 cup
freshly grated nutmeg	1.5 ml/¼ tsp
salt and freshly ground black pepper	
dried cannelloni tubes	8
béchamel sauce (see page 41)	300 ml/½ pint/1¼ cups
parmesan cheese	50 g/2 oz, grated
For the garlic mushrooms:	
olive oil	20 ml/1½ tbsp
garlic clove,	1, crushed
or garlic purée (paste)	5 ml/1 tsp
lemon juice	10 ml/2 tsp
small button mushrooms	300 g/11 oz

1 Put the spinach in a fine sieve (strainer) and drain well (don't squeeze out the liquid; it should be slightly wet). Place in a bowl with the ham or bacon, Ricotta, nutmeg, salt and pepper and mix well.

2 Spoon the mixture into the cannelloni tubes and arrange side by side in a shallow ovenproof dish (make sure that the dish fits in the halogen oven with a gap of at least 2.5 cm/1 in between it and the oven wall so the hot air can circulate).

3 Stir the sauce briefly, then spoon over the pasta in an even layer. Sprinkle the top with the Parmesan.

4 Whisk together the oil, garlic and lemon juice in a heatproof dish. Add the mushrooms and stir well to coat. Put on the low rack in the halogen oven.

5 Put the cannelloni on the high rack in the halogen oven and add the extender ring. Cook at 180°C/350°F for 45 minutes or until both the mushrooms and the cannelloni are tender when pierced with a knife and the top of the cannelloni is golden-brown and bubbling. If the top starts to over-brown during cooking, cover with foil.

steamed prawn and pork dumplings

Here little dumplings are served as a main meal with noodles, but they could also be a starter with chilli and soy dipping sauces.

SERVES 4
READY IN **45 MINUTES**

raw prawns	75 g/3 oz, finely chopped
minced (ground) pork	75 g/3 oz, finely chopped
spring onions (scallions)	2, finely sliced
fresh root ginger,	2 cm/¾ in piece, grated
or ginger purée (paste)	10 ml/2 tsp
dark soy sauce	15 ml/1 tbsp
dry sherry or rice wine	10 ml/2 tsp
toasted sesame oil	10 ml/2 tsp
salt	
wonton wrappers	16
oil	for greasing
broccoli	100 g/4 oz, cut into small sprigs
very hot water	250 ml/8 fl oz/1 cup
packet of ready-cooked rice noodles	300 g/11 oz
sweet chilli sauce	to serve

1 Put the chopped prawns and pork in a bowl with the spring onions, ginger, soy sauce, sherry or rice wine and 5 ml/1 tsp of the sesame oil. Season with a little salt and mix well.

2 Put rounded teaspoonfuls of the filling on the middle of each wonton wrapper. Dampen the edges lightly with water, then gather up the corners around the filling and pinch gently to seal.

3 Lightly grease the steamer tray and arrange the dumplings and sprigs of broccoli on it, leaving small spaces between each dumpling to allow the steam to circulate and to prevent them sticking together. Cover with a piece of lightly greased foil.

4 Pour the very hot water into the halogen oven bowl and position the low rack in the cooker. Place the steaming tray of dumplings on the rack. Switch on the halogen oven to 250°C/500°F and cook for 15 minutes or until the dumplings are cooked (cut one open to check).

5 Towards the end of the cooking time, put the noodles in a heatproof bowl and pour over enough boiling water to cover. Leave for a minute to heat through, then drain well and return to the bowl. Sprinkle the remaining sesame oil over the noodles and toss together.

6 Serve with the dumplings and broccoli. Accompany with sweet chilli sauce.

mixed fish casserole

Saffron gives this dish a beautiful golden colour and delicate flavour, but if it's too expensive use ground turmeric instead.

SERVES 4
READY IN **50 MINUTES**

large potato	1, cut into 2.5 cm/1 in chunks
onion	1, chopped
leek	1, thinly sliced
garlic cloves	3, finely chopped
olive oil	45 ml/3 tbsp
salt and freshly ground black pepper	
saffron threads	5 ml/1 tsp
can of chopped tomatoes	400 g/14 oz/large
sun-dried tomato paste	30 ml/2 tbsp
fish stock	150 ml/¼ pint/⅔ cup
bay leaves	2
mixed fish such as cod, haddock, halibut or bass	450 g/1 lb, skinned and cut into large chunks
raw prawns	225 g/8 oz
small baguette	1, cut into 2 cm/¾ in slices
butter	40 g/1½ oz/3 tbsp, softened

1 Toss together the potato, onion, leek, garlic and oil in an ovenproof casserole dish (Dutch oven) about 13 cm/5 in deep and 25 cm/10 in diameter. Season well with salt and pepper. Cook at 200°C/400°F on the high rack for 10 minutes, stirring a few times, until lightly browned.

2 Sprinkle the saffron over and stir in the tomatoes, tomato paste, stock and bay leaves. Cook for 10 minutes; the vegetables should be almost tender (if not, cook for a further 5 minutes).

3 Add the fish and cook for 5 minutes, then stir in the prawns and cook for a further 2–3 minutes or until the fish is opaque and flakes easily and the prawns are just pink.

4 Transfer the dish to the low rack and arrange the baguette slices on the high rack. Cook for 2–3 minutes until golden-brown, then turn and spread the untoasted side with the butter. Cook for a further 2 minutes until dark golden and serve straight away with the fish casserole.

spiced fish with noodles

Try this dish if you like lots of flavour but without the heat. Use light soy sauce if you prefer it to pungent nam pla sauce.

SERVES 4
READY IN **25 MINUTES, PLUS MARINATING**

garlic cloves	2, peeled
shallots	4, peeled
lemon grass stalk	1
red chilli	1, halved and seeded
or bottled ready- chopped chilli	5 ml/1 tsp
ground ginger	5 ml/1 tsp
ground turmeric	5 ml/1 tsp
nam pla (fish sauce)	15 ml/1 tbsp
sunflower oil	30 ml/2 tbsp
boneless white fish fillets	675 g/1½ lb, cut into eight pieces
salt and freshly ground black pepper	
packets of ready-cooked pad thai noodles	2 x 300 g/11 oz
boiling stock or water	30 ml/2 tbsp
a shredded cucumber and beansprout salad	to serve

1 Roughly chop the garlic, shallots, lemon grass and chilli and put in a food processor with the ginger, turmeric, nam pla and oil. Process to a smooth paste.

2 Put the fish in a bowl, add the paste and a little salt and pepper and gently turn until evenly coated. Cover and marinate at room temperature for 10–15 minutes.

3 Open the noodles and put them in an oven-proof dish. Sprinkle with the stock or water and cover tightly with pierced foil. Put on the low rack in the halogen oven.

4 Arrange the fish on a foil-lined baking tray. Put on the high rack and cook at 250°C/500°F for 8–10 minutes, turning carefully half-way through the cooking time, or until the top is lightly browned. Test for doneness by inserting a small knife and separating the flakes. Continue cooking for another minute or two, if necessary.

5 Check the noodles are piping hot (if necessary, cook uncovered for a minute or two on the low rack at 180°C/350°F) and pile on to warmed plates. Top with the spiced fish.

6 Serve straight away with a shredded cucumber and beansprout salad.

glamorgan brunch

Glamorgan sausages are a delicious vegetarian version enjoyed in Wales and are made from Caerphilly cheese and leeks.

 SERVES 4
READY IN 40 MINUTES V

For the cheese sausages:

butter	15 g/½ oz/1 tbsp
small leek	1, very finely chopped
eggs	2
milk	30 ml/2 tbsp
made mustard	2.5 ml/½ tsp
salt and freshly ground black pepper	
fresh white breadcrumbs	175 g/6 oz/3 cups
caerphilly cheese	100 g/4 oz, grated

For the roasted mushrooms and tomatoes:

sunflower oil	15 ml/1 tbsp
balsamic vinegar	10 ml/2 tsp
plum tomatoes	4, halved
small button mushrooms	225 g/8 oz

1 To make the cheese sausages, melt the butter in a saucepan on the hob, add the leek and cook gently for 5 minutes until soft. Turn off the heat and leave to cool for a few minutes.

2 Lightly beat together the eggs, milk and mustard in a bowl with a little salt and pepper. Stir in the breadcrumbs, followed by the leeks and cheese. Leave for a few minutes for the breadcrumbs to absorb the moisture, then divide the mixture into eight and shape into sausages. Chill until ready to cook.

3 Meanwhile, to prepare the mushrooms and tomatoes, whisk together the oil and vinegar in a bowl. Add the tomatoes and mushrooms and toss gently to coat in the mixture. Tip on to a baking tray, then make sure all the tomatoes are arranged cut-side up.

4 Cook on the low rack at 200°C/400°F for 10 minutes until lightly browned, turning the mushrooms half-way through the cooking time.

5 Add the high rack and extender ring. Arrange the sausages on a baking tray and cook on the high rack at 200°C/400°F for 10 minutes, turning frequently, so that they brown evenly. Serve with the mushrooms and tomatoes.

cheat's steak and kidney pie

If you've ever wondered why restaurant pie crusts are crisp and not soggy, here's their trick – the pastry is cooked separately.

SERVES 4
READY IN **1¾–2 HOURS**

lambs' kidneys	4
plain (all-purpose) flour	15 ml/1 tbsp
salt and freshly ground black pepper	
lean braising or stewing steak	550 g/1¼ lb, trimmed and cut into 2 cm/¾ in cubes
sunflower oil	45 ml/3 tbsp
onion	1, chopped
button mushrooms	175 g/6 oz, quartered
new potatoes	225 g/8 oz, quartered
red wine, port or extra stock	60 ml/4 tbsp
beef stock	300 ml/½ pint/1¼ cups
worcestershire sauce (optional)	10 ml/2 tsp
dried mixed herbs	2.5 ml/½ tsp
ready-rolled puff pastry (paste)	1 x 200 g/7 oz sheet
peas	to serve

1 Halve the kidneys, remove the white core, then cut them into 1 cm/½ in chunks. Mix the flour with a little salt and pepper and use this mixture to coat the beef.

2 Heat 30 ml/2 tbsp of the oil in a frying pan, add the beef and fry over a moderately high heat in two batches until browned all over. Transfer with a slotted spoon to a casserole dish (Dutch oven), making sure there is a gap of at least 2.5 cm/1 in between the dish and the oven wall so the hot air can circulate). Brown the kidneys in the remaining fat in the pan and add them to the beef.

3 Heat the remaining oil in the frying pan, add the onion and cook for 5 minutes. Add the mushrooms and potatoes and cook for 3–4 minutes, stirring frequently. Turn off the heat and stir in the red wine, port or extra stock.

4 Pour the mixture over the meat and stir in the stock, Worcestershire sauce, if using, and herbs. Cover with a lid or foil with a few holes pierced in it and cook at 160°C/325°F for 1¼–1½ hours or until the meat is tender.

5 About 20 minutes before the end of the cooking time, remove the puff pastry from the fridge and leave at room temperature for 5 minutes. Line a round halogen oven steaming tray measuring 23 cm/9 in across the base with a round of baking parchment. Place the high rack in the oven and turn up the temperature to 200°C/400°F.

6 Unroll the pastry and, using a plate as a guide, cut out a round slightly smaller than 23 cm/9 in. Place in the lined steaming tray and prick all over with a fork. Cut into four wedges (these will re-join as the pastry rise but the marks should be there for easy cutting when cooked). Cook for 5–6 minutes or until puffy and lightly browned.

7 Place a round baking tray the same size as the steaming tray over the pastry, then invert the pastry, uncooked side up, on to the baking tray and carefully peel away the baking parchment. Bake for a further 6–8 minutes or until well risen and brown.

8 Spoon the beef mixture on to warmed plates. Cut the pastry round into quarters and place a piece on top of each.

9 Serve with peas (if you don't want to cook these separately, they can be stirred into the beef mixture before cooking the pastry).

sweet treats

As well as main meals, you can create all sorts of cakes, cookies and delicious desserts in your halogen oven. Here, you'll find a selection of the best: crunchy-topped crumbles, crisp pastries and sticky and syrupy puddings. Cakes such as dark chocolate and carrot cake are superb; covered with foil throughout cooking, they turn out incredibly moist and full of flavour. Individual cupcakes and muffins can be made and baked in minutes; perfect if you want just a small batch. These should be made in silicone cake cases as you'll find paper ones will wilt and lose their shape during baking.

Check cakes are cooked through by lightly pressing with a finger; they should be firm and slightly springy. When done, turn off the temperature and leave in the oven for a few minutes to finish cooking and cool and settle a little before removing. And, if you love meringues, the Thaw/Wash setting on the halogen oven cooks them to perfection; crisp and white on the outside with the softest moist marshmallow middle.

tropical fruit crumble

Forget apple crumble! This tropical fruit version is so easy to prepare as it uses canned fruits, taking only seconds to slice.

SERVES 4
READY IN **40 MINUTES**

can of pineapple chunks or pieces	200 g/7 oz/small
sultanas (golden raisins) or chopped dates	25 g/1 oz/3 tbsp
dark rum or extra pineapple juice from the can	30 ml/2 tbsp
wholemeal or plain (all-purpose) flour	100 g/4 oz/1 cup
ground cinnamon	2.5 ml/½ tsp
ground ginger	2.5 ml/½ tsp
butter	65 g/2½ oz/generous ¼ cup
desiccated (shredded) coconut	30 ml/2 tbsp
light brown sugar	45 ml/3 tbsp
large firm ripe bananas	2
ice-cream or crème fraîche	to serve

1 Drain the pineapple, reserving the juice. Put the sultanas in a bowl with 30 ml/2 tbsp of the pineapple juice and the rum or extra pineapple juice. Leave to soak for a few minutes while preparing the crumble topping and fruit.

2 Sift the flour, cinnamon and ginger into a bowl, adding any bran left in the sieve (strainer) if you used wholemeal flour. Dice the butter and rub into the flour until the mixture resembles breadcrumbs. Stir in the coconut and 30ml/2 tbsp of the sugar.

3 Peel the bananas and cut into 2 cm/¾ in slices. Add to the soaked sultanas and juice with the drained pineapple. Sprinkle the remaining sugar over and stir together. Tip into an ovenproof dish and spread out evenly.

4 Sprinkle the crumble mixture over the top of the fruit. Cover the dish with pierced foil and bake on the lower rack of the halogen oven at 200°C/400°F for 25 minutes, removing the foil for the last 5 minutes to allow the top to brown.

5 Serve hot or warm with vanilla or coconut-ice cream or crème fraîche.

sticky syrup sponges

The halogen oven is better suited to cooking individual sponge puddings than large ones. Use small basins or ramekins.

MAKES 4
READY IN **50 MINUTES**

butter, preferably unsalted (sweet) softened, plus extra for greasing	100 g/4 oz/½ cup
golden (light corn) or maple syrup	90 ml/6 tbsp
light brown sugar	100 g/4 oz/½ cup
self-raising flour	100 g/4 oz/1 cup
eggs	2, lightly beaten
hot (not boiling) water	250 ml/8 fl oz/1 cup
custard or ice-cream	to serve

1 Lightly grease four 175 ml/6 fl oz/¾ cup metal pudding basins or ramekins (custard cups) with softened butter. Divide the syrup between them.

2 Put the butter and sugar in a bowl and beat together. Sift the flour over and add the eggs. Beat again until combined. Divide the sponge mixture between the basins, then cover each tightly with pierced foil.

3 Put the low rack into the halogen oven and pour the hot water into the halogen oven bowl.

4 Place the puddings on the rack and cook at 180°C/ 350°F for 35 minutes or until the sponges are cooked (a fine skewer inserted into the middle of a pudding should come out clean). Turn out.

5 Serve hot with custard or ice-cream.

saucy lemon pudding

Give this retro favourite a revival and watch in the halogen oven as it separates into lemon custard with a light sponge topping.

SERVES 4
READY IN **45 MINUTES**

butter	75 g/3 oz/generous ⅓ cup, plus extra for greasing
plain (all-purpose) flour	75 g/3 oz/¾ cup
caster (superfine) sugar	150 g/5 oz/generous ½ cup
full-fat milk	350 ml/12 fl oz/1⅓ cups
eggs	3, separated
lemons	2, finely grated zest only
lemon juice	100 ml/3½ fl oz/scant ½ cup
crème fraîche	to serve

1 Lightly grease an ovenproof dish. Sift the flour and 100 g/4 oz/½ cup of the sugar into a bowl. Put the butter and about 150 ml/¼ pint/⅔ cup of the milk into a pan and heat on the hob until the butter has melted.

2 Stir in the remaining milk and the egg yolks. Add the milk mixture to the dry ingredients with the lemon zest and juice and stir together.

3 Whisk the egg whites until soft peaks form. Whisk in the remaining sugar a tablespoonful at a time until the mixture is thick and glossy. Gently fold into the lemon mixture. Pour into the prepared dish.

4 Place the dish on the low rack in the halogen oven, then pour hot water into the halogen oven bowl until it comes about 1 cm/½ in up the sides of the dish.

5 Cook at 175°C/340°F for 30 minutes or until the pudding is firm and spongy on top but still soft and sauce-like at the bottom.

6 Serve hot or warm with crème fraîche.

berries and cream meringues

The halogen oven makes perfect white meringues on the Thaw/Wash setting; crisp on the outside and soft in the middle.

MAKES 6
READY IN **1 HOUR**

For the meringues:

egg whites	2, at room temperature
caster (superfine) sugar	100 g/4 oz/½ cup

For the filling:

double (heavy) or whipping cream	150 ml/¼ pint/⅔ cup
vanilla essence (extract)	2.5 ml/½ tsp
berries such as small strawberries, raspberries and blueberries	175 g/6 oz

1 To make the meringues, line a baking (cookie) sheet with baking parchment. Whisk the egg whites until they form soft peaks when the whisk is removed. Add the sugar a heaped teaspoonful at a time, whisking for a few seconds between each addition, until all the sugar is added; the mixture should look glossy and stiff.

2 Scoop the mixture into six mounds on the baking sheet then, using the back of a teaspoon, make a shallow hollow in the middle of each meringue.

3 Put the meringues on the low rack in the halogen oven and cook at 125°C/250°F for 5 minutes. Lower the heat to the Thaw/Wash setting and cook for a further 40 minutes until the meringue is firm. Turn off the heat and allow the meringues to cool completely in the oven, then carefully peel the meringues away from the baking parchment.

4 To make the filling, whisk the cream and vanilla in a small bowl until it forms soft peaks. Spoon into the hollows in the meringue nests and top with prepared berries, piling them high. Serve within 15 minutes of filling.

pear puffs with streusel topping

Although it can be difficult to get the bottom of pastry to cook, this can be solved by turning it over part-way through cooking.

MAKES 4
READY IN 40 MINUTES

ready-rolled puff pastry (paste)	1 x 200 g/7 oz sheet
plain (all-purpose) flour	25 g/1 oz/¼ cup
ground cinnamon	2.5 ml/½ tsp
butter	20 g/¾ oz
caster (superfine) sugar	45 ml/3 tbsp
cornflour (cornstarch)	7.5 ml/1½ tsp
firm ripe pears	2, peeled, cored and thinly sliced
ice-cream, crème fraîche or custard	to serve

1 Preheat the halogen oven to 200°C/400°F. Take the puff pastry out of the fridge and leave at room temperature for a few minutes (this makes it less likely to crack).

2 For the topping, put the flour and cinnamon in a bowl. Dice the butter and rub into the flour until the mixture resembles fine breadcrumbs. Stir in 15 ml/1 tbsp of the sugar, then gather the mixture together to make a dough and gently squeeze it into a ball. Coarsely grate the dough and set aside.

3 Unroll the pastry and cut out a 20 cm/8 in round, using a plate as a guide. Cut the round into quarters to make four wedge shapes. Transfer to a round baking (cookie) sheet at least 23 cm/9 in across, spacing the pieces slightly apart to allow them room to rise. Prick each pastry triangle several times with a fork.

4 Mix together the remaining sugar and the cornflour in a bowl. Add the pear slices and toss to coat evenly (keep tossing until all the sugar and cornflour are soaked up), then arrange on top of the pastry triangles, leaving a 1 cm/½ in pastry rim. Sprinkle the crumble mixture over the pears.

5 Cook in the halogen oven for about 8 minutes or until the pastry is well risen and crisp and both the topping and the pastry are golden-brown. Turn off the oven and leave for at least 10 minutes or until you are ready to serve (this allows the very hot sugary topping to cool and set).

6 Turn the pastries over and cook the bases for 3–4 minutes or until lightly browned and crisp.

7 Serve them topping-side up with ice-cream, crème fraîche or custard.

white chocolate and raspberry muffins

So easy to prepare but so delicious!
White chocolate chunks and sweetly tart
raspberries are a wonderful combination.

MAKES 6
READY IN **30 MINUTES**

self-raising flour	150 g/5 oz/1¼ cups
baking powder	2.5 ml/½ tsp
salt	a pinch
butter	25 g/1 oz/2 tbsp
caster (superfine) sugar	40 g/1½ oz/1½ tbsp
fresh or frozen (do not thaw first) raspberries	75 g/3 oz
white chocolate	75 g/3 oz, coarsely chopped
lemon (optional)	½, finely grated zest only
egg	1, lightly beaten
milk	120 ml/4 fl oz/½ cup

1 Put the low rack in the halogen oven and preheat to 200°C/400°F. Arrange 6 silicone cupcake or muffin cases (don't use paper ones as they would be blown over by the fan) on a round baking (cookie) sheet.

2 Sift the flour, baking powder and salt into a large bowl. Dice the butter and rub into the mixture until it resembles fine breadcrumbs. Stir in the sugar, raspberries, chocolate and lemon zest, if using.

3 In a separate bowl or jug, mix together the egg and milk, then pour the egg mixture all at once into the dry ingredients and mix briefly until just combined.

4 Spoon the mixture into the silicone cases, dividing evenly. Bake for 5 minutes, then lower the temperature to 175°C/340°F and bake for a further 12–15 minutes or until the muffins are well risen, golden and just firm.

5 Turn off the halogen oven and leave the muffins for 2 minutes before removing. Transfer to a wire rack and serve warm or cold.

frosted carrot cake

A wonderfully moist and nutty carrot cake with a creamy smooth frosting slightly sharpened with a touch of lemon juice.

SERVES 6–8
READY IN **1¼ HOURS**

For the cake:

walnuts or pecan nuts	75 g/3 oz/¾ cup
butter	for greasing
small orange	1
light soft brown sugar	100 g/4 oz/½ cup
sunflower oil	120 ml/4 fl oz/½ cup
eggs	2, lightly beaten
self-raising flour	150 g/5 oz/1¼ cups
bicarbonate of soda (baking soda)	3.5 ml/¾ tsp
ground cinnamon	5 ml/1 tsp
finely grated carrot	175 g/6 oz (about 2 carrots)

For the frosting:

butter	40 g/1½ oz/3 tbsp, softened
icing (confectioners') sugar	40 g/1½ oz/¼ cup, sifted
full-fat soft cheese	75 g/3 oz/scant ½ cup
lemon juice	5 ml/1 tsp

1 To make the cake, put the nuts on a baking (cookie) sheet and place on the low rack. Turn on the halogen oven to 175°C/340°F and toast the nuts for 4–5 minutes (watch them as they burn easily and take them out if they start to over-brown). Remove from the oven and roughly chop when cool enough to handle.

2 Grease the base of a deep 18 cm/7 in round cake tin and line with baking parchment. Finely grate the zest from the orange and set aside, then squeeze the juice and reserve.

3 Put the sugar and oil in a bowl and beat with a wooden spoon or electric whisk for a minute, breaking down any lumps of sugar. Add the eggs one at a time, whisking well after each addition.

4 Sift the flour, bicarbonate of soda and cinnamon over the mixture and start to fold in. When it is nearly mixed, add the carrot, nuts and 15 ml/1 tbsp of the orange juice and the zest and continue folding and stirring until well mixed.

5 Pour the mixture into the prepared tin and cover tightly with foil. Bake on the low rack for 50 minutes. Remove the foil and bake for a further 5–10 minutes, until the middle of the cake is firm and a skewer comes out clean when pushed into the centre of the cake.

6 Remove from the oven and leave to cool in the tin for 20 minutes. Turn out on to a wire rack and leave to cool completely.

7 Meanwhile, to make the frosting, put the butter and sugar in a bowl and beat together until smooth. Beat in the soft cheese and lemon juice. Spread evenly over the top of the cake. Store in an airtight container in the fridge.

dark chocolate cake

Darkly delicious, with a rich flavour though not overly sweet. Cover with bought frosting instead of icing sugar, if you prefer.

SERVES 6–8
READY IN 1¼ HOURS

soft light brown sugar	100 g/4 oz/½ cup
golden (light corn) syrup	45 ml/3 tbsp
plain yoghurt	100 ml/3½ fl oz/scant ½ cup
sunflower oil	100 ml/3½ fl oz/scant ½ cup
eggs	2, lightly beaten
self-raising flour	150 g/5 oz/1¼ cups
cocoa (unsweetened chocolate) powder	45 ml/3 tbsp
salt	a pinch
bicarbonate of soda (baking soda)	2.5 ml/½ tsp
icing (confectioner's) sugar	15 ml/1 tbsp
whipped cream or crème fraîche	to serve

1 Preheat the halogen oven to 175°C/340°F. Grease the base of a deep 18 cm/7 in round cake tin and line with baking parchment.

2 Put the sugar, syrup, yoghurt, oil and eggs in a mixing bowl and stir with a wooden spoon or wire whisk until blended.

3 Sift the flour, cocoa, salt and bicarbonate of soda over the egg mixture and gently stir in. Pour into the prepared tin and cover the top tightly with foil.

4 Bake on the low rack for 50 minutes to 1 hour or until a skewer comes out clean when pushed into the centre of the cake.

5 Remove from the oven and leave to cool in the tin for 20 minutes. Turn out on to a wire rack and leave to cool completely.

6 Dust with icing sugar and serve with whipped cream or crème fraîche.

cinnamon rock cakes

You could use cocoa powder and chocolate chips instead of cinnamon and fruit. These cakes are best on the day they are cooked.

MAKES ABOUT 6
READY IN **20 MINUTES**

self-raising flour	175 g/6 oz/1½ cups
ground cinnamon	5 ml/1 tsp
baking powder	5 ml/1 tsp
soft margarine	75 g/3 oz/3 tbsp, chilled
granulated or caster (superfine) sugar	25 g/1 oz/2 tbsp
mixed dried fruit (fruit cake mix) (a 'luxury' mix is ideal)	100 g/4 oz/¾ cup
egg	1
milk	15 ml/1 tbsp
demerara or granulated sugar	15 ml/1 tbsp

1 Sift the flour, cinnamon and baking powder into a mixing bowl. Rub in the margarine until the mixture resembles breadcrumbs.

2 Stir in the granulated or caster sugar and fruit, then make a hollow in the middle. Beat together the egg and milk and pour into the hollow. Stir the mixture together to make a rough, lumpy mixture (do not over-mix).

3 Put the low rack in the halogen oven and preheat to 200°C/400°F. Using two spoons, shape the mixture into about six rough mounds on a lightly greased baking (cookie) sheet. Sprinkle with the demerara or granulated sugar.

4 Bake for 5 minutes, then lower the heat to 150°C/300°F and bake for a further 5 minutes or until the tops are well browned and the cakes are cooked through. Leave on the baking tray for a few minutes, then transfer to a wire rack. Serve warm or cold. Eat on the day of making.

index